Creative Themes for Every Day

Carson-Dellosa Publishing LLC
Greensboro, North Carolina

- Before beginning any food activity, ask families' permission and inquire about students' food allergies and religious or other food restrictions.

- Before beginning any nature activity, ask families' permission and inquire about students' plant and animal allergies. Remind students not to touch potentially harmful plants during the activity.

- Nature activities may require adult supervision. Before beginning any nature activity, ask parents' permission and inquire about the student's plant and animal allergies. Remind the student not to touch plants or animals during the activity without adult supervision.

- Never leave students unattended around a hot lamp. Touching a hot lightbulb can cause burns.

- Keep boiling water away from students.

- Before beginning any feather activity, inquire about students' allergies.

Credits

Content Editor: Joanie Oliphant

Copy Editor: Beatrice Allen

Layout Design: Lori Jackson

Carson-Dellosa Publishing LLC
PO Box 35665
Greensboro, NC 27425 USA
www.carsondellosa.com

Printed in the USA . All rights reserved.

1 2 3 4 5 GLO 15 14 13 12 11

ISBN 978-1-936024-82-7

335107784

Table of Contents

Introduction

Welcome to *Creative Themes for Every Day!* If you have chosen this book, chances are that you have decided to do what many preschool teachers have done successfully before you: organize your classroom teaching by themes. There are many reasons why using themes in preschool classrooms is such a popular and successful method. First, themes make sense to young students. Preschoolers crave the comfort of predictability. Knowing that they can revisit a favorite activity if they choose, or that a favorite theme will be around for a while, gives them a sense of security and the time and freedom to repeat an activity or reread a favorite book. Themes also make it possible to relate your classroom to things that are going on outside of school, such as changing seasons and upcoming holidays. Echoing what is going on outside of the classroom helps students make connections and reinforces their classroom learning. Finally, themes help you keep your classroom manageable. Organizing your materials by theme allows you to remove some unrelated items. Storing related items together can help you keep clutter under control and also help you introduce new items and retire others as themes change. Inside this book, you will find everything you need to teach 20 popular preschool themes that are sure to keep each student motivated to learn. Each theme includes a literature list, activities covering multiple concept areas, complete teacher directions, letters home, and necessary reproducible patterns. Below are some suggestions for how to use this book to make the most of your classroom time.

Centers

Many of the activities in this book can be used with a whole class or small groups, but you can also set up many activities at centers. Consider providing centers for art, dramatic play, blocks, math and manipulatives, reading and writing, and science. These basic centers can be adapted to include other subject areas, like social studies and music, as needed. To make the most of your centers when following these themes, read the activities of the theme that you are preparing to teach, then stock your centers with the appropriate materials to create easy transitions for students and peace of mind for yourself. If you store excess items in plastic bins labeled with theme names, you can easily rotate the bins as themes change.

Literature Selections

A list of books that relate to each theme can be found in each introduction. Read the book descriptions and introductions for helpful ideas about how to use the literature selections. Also, use the themes to sort and classify books that you already have. If you have limited space, store your books in a remote location. At the beginning of each theme, retrieve related titles. Create a portable book nook by placing the books in a large wicker basket or a box. Store the basket of related books in your literacy center and replace those books with new ones when you have finished with that theme. Send home the literature list at the back of the book to help parents make relevant book selections at home.

Me, Myself, and My Friends

Students love to share information about themselves, as well as learn about others. This theme can help students appreciate their uniqueness and can help make them feel special through role-playing activities, finger plays, songs, and games. This theme is effective when used to help students get to know each other better. It can also be valuable to incorporate activities like Body Glue (page 8) and Match and Wiggle (page 8) after students know each other well to remind them to appreciate each other. Use the self-esteem-themed books below at any time, but especially when students are having a hard time getting along. This section includes ideas for finding out more about each student's talents and preferences. Just as Little Critter does in *This Is My Body* by Gina and Mercer Mayer (Golden Books, 2000), matching and movement activities in this section help each student become more aware of how his body can move.

Literature Selections

Bear's New Friend by Karma Wilson (Simon & Schuster, 2006). Bear welcomes a shy new forest friend. The story is filled with charming rhyme and rich illustrations.

How Are You Peeling? by Joost Elffers and Saxton Freymann (Scholastic Paperbacks, 2004). Expressive vegetable sculptures accompany a subtle, refreshing poem that deals with many of the happy and not-so-happy feelings that arise from interacting with others.

I Like Myself! by Karen Beaumont (Harcourt Children's Books, 2004). The main character in this book likes herself because there is just no one else like her. Fun illustrations and charming, playful text make this a memorable ode to self-esteem.

I'm Gonna Like Me: Letting Off a Little Self-Esteem by Jamie Lee Curtis (HarperCollins, 2002). Follow two quirky cartoon kids through their day as they learn to like themselves—even when they are not quite perfect. Kids will love the exuberant art and rhythmic text.

This Is My Body by Gina and Mercer Mayer (Golden Books, 2000). Little Critter, the familiar, beloved character, offers a low-key introduction to body parts, including his mouth, legs, and even fur.

We Are All Alike . . . We Are All Different by The Cheltenham Elementary School Kindergartners (Scholastic Paperbacks, 2002). Celebrate diversity and differences while demonstrating that in important ways, students are not so different after all.

Fingerprint Exploration

Materials: ink pads with washable ink, index cards, crayons, white paper, magnifying glasses

Find 8 to 10 volunteers. Have each volunteer make a fingerprint on two index cards. Each volunteer should use the same finger when making the prints. Code the cards on the backs so that students will be able to match them. For example, on the back of each of one volunteer's cards, draw a red dot; on the back of each of another volunteer's cards, draw a blue square, etc. Place the cards and supplies on a table in the center. Talk to students about how fingerprints are made and explain that everyone's fingerprints are unique. Let students use the ink pads to make several more fingerprints on the white paper. Then, after students have washed their hands, let them examine the fingerprint cards with the magnifying glasses. Have students try to find the matching cards by comparing the prints. Have students check their answers by comparing the color-coded dots on the backs of the cards.

My Name Is Special

Materials: letter stamps, ink pads with washable ink, paper

Write each student's name at the top of a sheet of paper. If desired, use the Internet or a baby name book to research the meaning of each student's name and write it at the bottom of the sheet of paper. Place the supplies on a table in the center. When students come to the center, have them find their sheet of paper. Then, talk to them about how special their names are. If you included the meanings of their names, discuss that information as well. Let each student use the letter stamps to spell his name on the sheet of paper while using the written name as a guide. Students can also spell the names of friends, family members, or pets using the stamps.

Plain Old Me!

Sing or chant "Plain Old Me!" as you perform the finger play with students.

Plain Old Me!

I have 10 fingers. (wiggle fingers)

I have 10 toes. (wiggle toes)

I have two hands, and two ears, and a nose. (shake hands, touch ears, and point to nose)

I have some hair, (place hands on head)

And a face you see, (open hands on the sides of cheeks around face)

But the best thing I have . . .

Is plain old me! (point to chest)

Mirror, Mirror

Materials: one small plastic mirror per student

Talk about students' differences and similarities. Name an attribute, such as black hair, and have each student with that attribute do something, such as stand up, to identify herself. Repeat with several different attributes, like hair color, height, color of clothing, eye color, length of hair, hair style, gender, age, etc. Give each student small plastic mirrors. Have students look at themselves closely. Allow students to talk to each other about what they see in the mirror. Call attention to different things as they look. Ask, "What colors do you see in your eyes? What direction are the hairs on your eyebrows going? Is the color of your skin the same on your face and hands? Do you have freckles? Can you count them? Does your eyelid cover part of your iris? Do you see your teeth when you smile? Are your lips shaped the same on the top and bottom? Side to side?" Be sure to discuss all features and differences positively.

Body Glue

Materials: Body Parts Cards (pages 13–14), crayons or markers, scissors, hat or box

Make copies of the Body Parts Cards. Color, cut out, and laminate the cards as desired. Place all of the Body Parts Cards in a hat or box and mix them. (You may want to remove cards for body parts that are above the shoulders.) Draw two cards from the hat or box. Tell students that today you have special body glue and pretend to apply it to students. Whichever body parts you draw from the hat will be "glued" together. Each time a new set of body parts is drawn from the hat, the glue can be separated to create a new bond. For example, if the knee and elbow cards are drawn, students must glue their elbows to their knees and stay that way until you tell them to break the bond and get ready for the next set of cards.

Extension: Have students work together as partners. (You may want to remove cards that could make students uncomfortable.) This time, the bond of glue cannot be broken. Draw two cards from the hat. For example, if you draw the hand card and the foot card, one partner should "glue" his hand to the partner's foot. Draw two more cards. Have students glue those two parts together, being careful not to break the existing bond between the hand and the foot. Continue playing until all students are completely glued together. For a challenge, specify right or left for paired body parts, such as hands, feet, elbows, knees, etc.

Match and Wiggle

Materials: Body Parts Cards (pages 13–14), music

Enlarge the Body Parts Cards for easier viewing. As you introduce each card, have each student match the body part on the card to her own body part, without verbally identifying them. For example, if you hold up the hand card, students should wiggle only their hands to signify that they recognize and can match the card by their movements. Repeat for other body parts or introduce more than one card at a time. If you wish, play music during this activity to add a beat for wiggling.

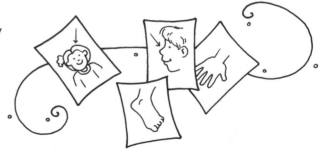

Wiggle Those Piggies

Have students remove their shoes and socks for this activity. Point, count, and wiggle each finger and toe while singing "Ten Little Piggies."

Ten Little Piggies

One little, two little, three little piggies,

Four little, five little, six little piggies,

Seven little, eight little, nine little piggies,

Ten little piggy fingers!

One little, two little, three little piggies,

Four little, five little, six little piggies,

Seven little, eight little, nine little piggies,

Ten little piggy toes!

Body Patterns

Using the AAABB pattern, have students perform the actions as you say the pattern. After doing those given here, invite each student to come up with different body motions.

Clap, clap, clap (clap hands three times),

Stomp, stomp (stomp feet twice).

Clap, clap, clap,

Stomp, stomp.

Hear, hear, hear (touch ears three times),

Wiggle, wiggle (wiggle body twice).

Hear, hear, hear,

Wiggle, wiggle.

Shake, shake, shake (shake hands three times),

Smack, smack (smack lips twice).

Shake, shake, shake,

Smack, smack.

Nod, nod, nod (nod head three times),

Knee, knee (tap knees twice).

Nod, nod, nod,

Knee, knee.

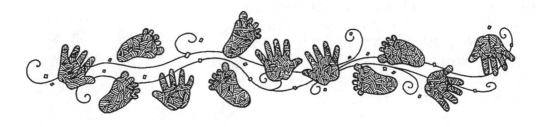

My Senses Help Me

Sing to the tune of "The Farmer in the Dell." Point to each body part as it is named.

My Senses Help Me

My eyes help me see.
My eyes help me see.
We use our eyes
For color and size;
My eyes help me see.

My ears help me hear.
My ears help me hear.
Sounds high or low
Or loud or soft;
My ears help me hear.

My nose helps me smell.
My nose helps me smell.
Flowers so sweet,
And stinky feet;
My nose helps me smell.

My hands help me feel.
My hands help me feel.
Hot or cold,
Smooth or rough;
My hands help me feel.

My mouth helps me taste.
My mouth helps me taste.
Sweet and salty,
Sour and bitter;
My mouth helps me taste.

My Family

Materials: a picture of your family, copies of the Frame Pattern (page 12)

Share a photograph of your family and describe who is in the picture. Talk about names, ages, and family activities. Then, ask students to talk about their families. Lead the discussion by saying things like, "Raise your hand if you are the oldest child in your family." Guide students to discover that families come in many different configurations, and that a family is a group of people who live together and care about (and for) each other. Give students copies of the Frame Pattern and have them draw pictures of their families. Ask students to think of one thing that they like about their families. Then, ask each student to tell his neighbor something that he likes. When everyone has shared, take turns around the circle and listen to each student tell about his family.

Let's Wash

Materials: music

Play music while students use their hands to pretend that they are washing. Allow about fifteen seconds for students to act out each suggestion.

Let's Wash

Let's wash our faces.

Let's wash our hands.

Let's wash our feet.

Let's wash our backs.

Let's wash our knees.

Let's wash our elbows.

Let's wash our ears.

Let's wash our hair.

Let's wash all over.

Switched-Up Twist-Up

Materials: four colorful dot stickers per student, construction paper, glue, wooden craft sticks

Hand four different colorful stickers to each student. Have students place a red sticker on their left hand, a yellow sticker on their right hand, a green sticker on their left foot, and a blue sticker on their right foot. Create two, two-sided flags to use as signals. Cut out four construction paper rectangles, one in each color. Glue the red rectangle to the yellow rectangle with a craft stick handle in the middle. Do the same with the blue and green rectangles. Use the colorful flags to signal which body part students should raise. For example, show them the yellow flag, and make sure that students raise their right hands. Repeat with the other three colors to make sure that everyone knows which hand or foot to move. Flash the flags more and more quickly while students try to match your signals.

Extension: Repeat the activity using other body parts, such as the head, knees, hips, etc. Each time you hold up a flag, announce a movement, such as, "Shake," and have students match body parts and actions.

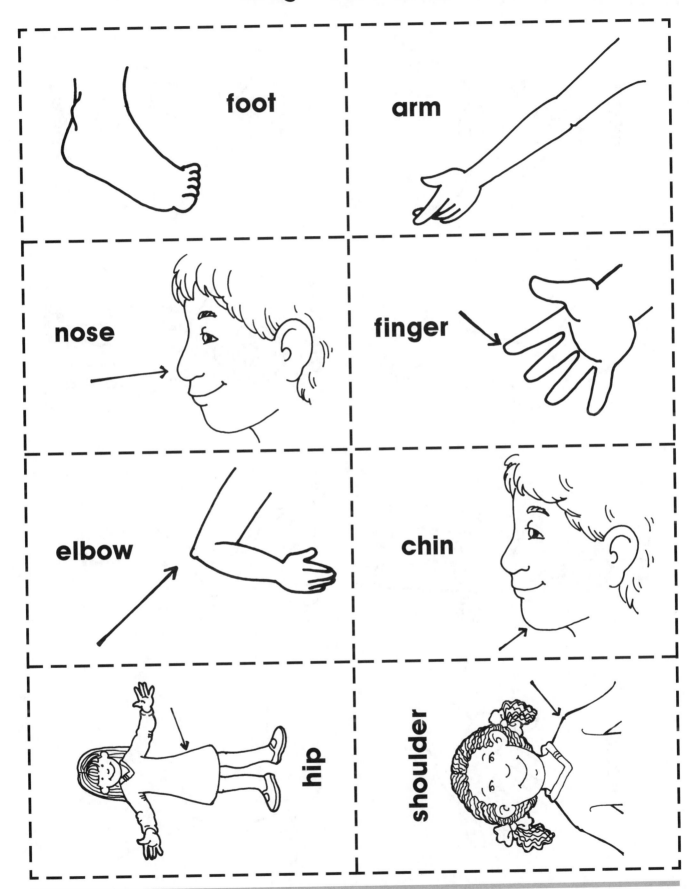

foot

arm

nose

finger

elbow

chin

hip

shoulder

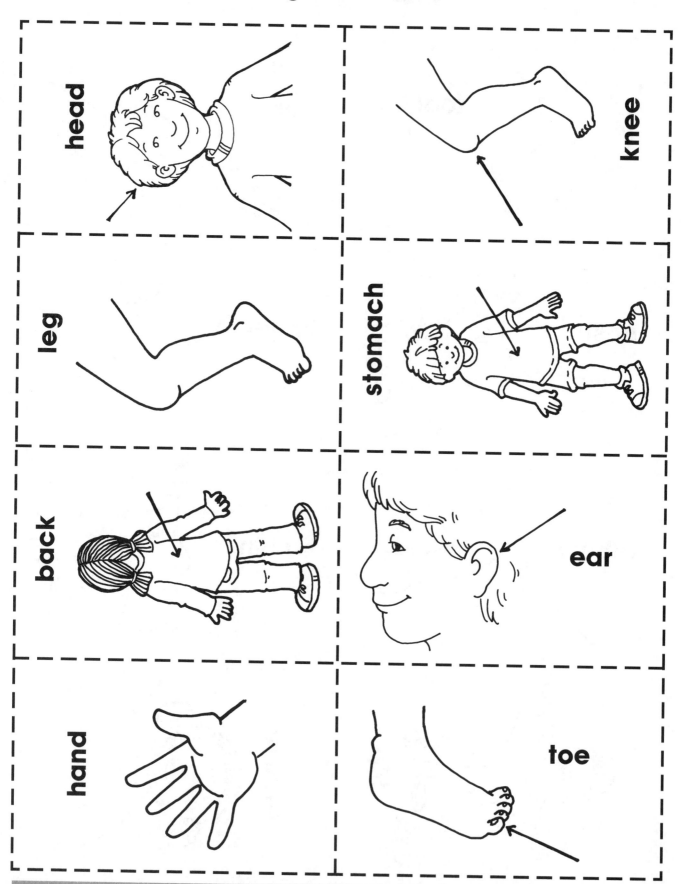

head

knee

leg

stomach

back

ear

hand

toe

Me, Myself, and My Friends

Dear Family Members,

Children love to learn about themselves and their friends. During our "Me, Myself, and My Friends" unit, children are learning more about what they like and what they can do. They are sharing their preferences and showing off their many skills and talents. Our "Me, Myself, and My Friends" activities help children:

- Engage socially with each other and with teachers
- Contribute to the classroom community
- Use language to communicate their thoughts
- Learn new things about their friends
- Feel great about themselves

You can use these activities at home to encourage your child's journey of self-discovery.

- Ask your child, "What is your favorite book?" Then, ask why it is his favorite and read it together. (Do not be surprised if the favorite book changes often.)
- Have a funny face contest. Stand in front of a mirror with your child. Ask her to make a funny face, and try to make the same face. Then, it is your turn.
- Empower your child with a game of Follow the Leader. Either play the traditional way, or play some dance music and follow your child's moves. Let him name his moves, like "The William Wiggle."
- If you have a class picture, sit with your child and ask about her friends. Let your child point to each friend and tell you something about that classmate. If your child has trouble, ask questions like, "What does Stella bring for lunch?" or "What games does Martin like to play?"

Thank you for sharing your child with us!

Sincerely,

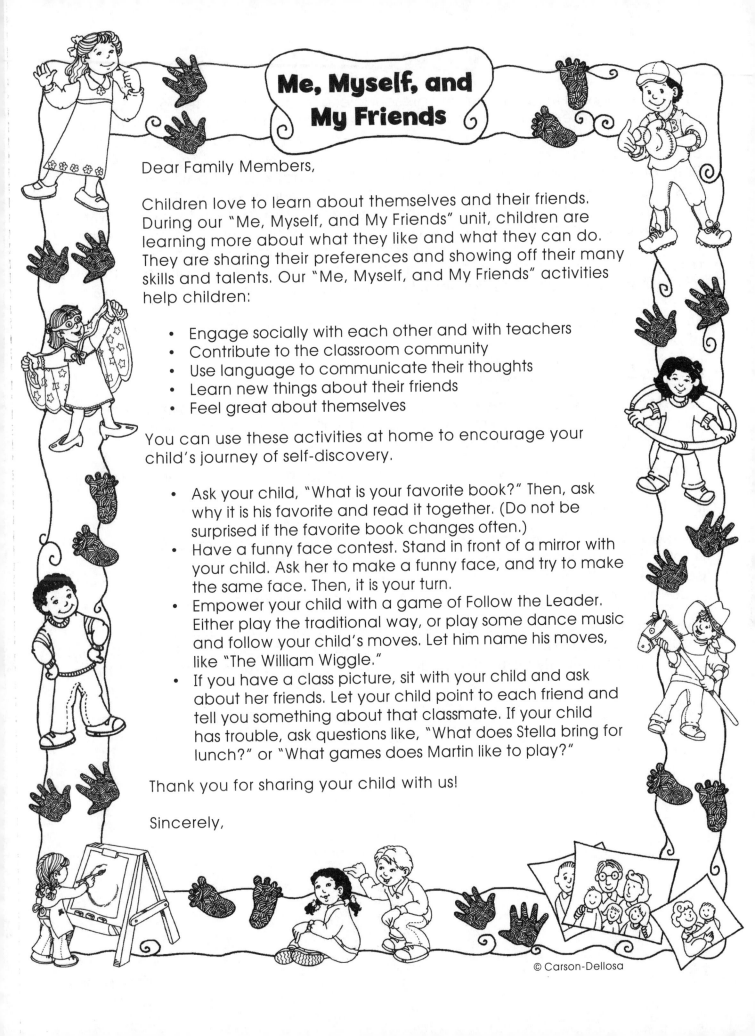

We Love Our Pets!

Animals bring out the best in many preschoolers. Students are often proud of their family pets, and enjoy helping to care for them. Give each student opportunities in the classroom to celebrate pet ownership. For example, let them celebrate acquiring a pet by creating a pet shop. Make some "Pet Treats" snacks to share. Play some silly, pet-themed games. And, find out what kinds of pets each student has to sneak in some graphing. If some students in your classroom do not have pets, encourage them to celebrate their favorite stuffed animals that sleep with them, ride to school (and sometimes come into the school) with them, and comfort them much as a live pet would. Treating the stuffed animals like real pets may also give you an opportunity to help students discover some animals not otherwise found in the pet realm. Use *Pet Show!* to inspire a classroom pet show. Include the other literature selections to spark discussion about how students got their pets. *Franklin Wants a Pet* is a good choice for comparing and contrasting different kinds of pets.

Literature Selections

The Best Pet of All by David LaRochelle (Dutton Juvenile, 2004). A boy who wants a dog brings home a messy dragon instead, so that the dog seems like a great trade-up to the boy's reluctant mother.

Birthday Pet by Ellen Javernick (Marshall Cavendish Corporation, 2009). Danny wants a pet turtle for his birthday, but his parents have a different idea. The illustrations are fun and engaging.

Franklin Wants a Pet by Paulette Bourgeois (Scholastic Paperbacks, 1995). Franklin (the turtle from the ever-popular series) desperately wants a pet. His parents are not keen on the idea, but Franklin pleasantly surprises them with his determination, sense of responsibility, and eventual choice of a pet.

The Perfect Pet by Margie Palatini (Katherine Tegen Books, 2003). After unsuccessfully springing pet after pet on her parents, who adamantly do not want a pet, Elizabeth finally befriends a bug named Doug and makes him part of the family.

Pet Show! by Ezra Jack Keats (Puffin, 2001). Archie wants to enter his cat in the neighborhood pet show. But, when his cat disappears, Archie must find a new way to enter the pet show—and he must find his cat too!

Pet Treats for People

Materials: bowls of cereal flakes (fish), pretzel sticks (dogs), fish-shaped crackers (cats), gummy bugs (reptiles and amphibians), sunflower seeds (rodents), dried apricots, banana chips, and apple chips (birds), green food coloring and coconut (rabbits), spoon for each bowl, resealable plastic bags

Pour each type of snack into a bowl. Mix the green food coloring with the coconut to represent the grass that rabbits eat. Label each bowl with the type of animal and food that it represents. Place all of the supplies on a table.

Have students create bags of "Pet Treats." Explain that the foods in the bowls represent foods that pets eat. But, instead of sharing with their pets, students will get to enjoy these treats themselves. Explain the steps to students as you demonstrate the activity. Each student should then follow the recipe.

1. Have each student place one spoonful of each type of snack in his bag.
2. Help each student seal the bag and shake it gently to mix the treats.
3. Let students enjoy their snacks!

 **(See page 2.)**

Pet Graph

Materials: Pet Cards (page 26), scissors, crayons or markers, bulletin board paper, index cards, glue sticks

Make several copies of the Pet Cards. Cut apart the cards and sort them by animal type. Draw a blank bar graph, with an x-axis and a y-axis, on bulletin board paper. Place the graph on a table in a center or hang it on a wall or bulletin board where students can reach it. Place the other supplies on a table near the graph. Have each student select a card for each pet she has at home. For example, if a student has two dogs and three fish, she should take two dog cards and three fish cards. Let students color the cards. If a student's pet is not featured on a card, provide a blank index card and help her draw a picture of her pet. Or, if a student does not have any pets, have her select or make cards for pets that she would like to have or for her favorite stuffed animals. When students are finished coloring, have them glue the cards in rows on the graph to show which types of pets they have. Identify the most and least common kinds of pets.

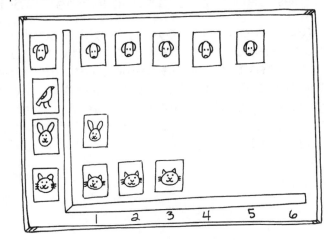

Puppy Song

Sing to the tune of "Jack and Jill" as you do the motions with students.

Puppy Song

Mom and Dad, please let me keep	(arms out at sides, as if pleading)
This puppy I have met.	(hugging a puppy)
He needs a home,	
I'm all alone,	(fists rubbing eyes)
I'll take good care of my pet.	(hands on hips)

Where Has My Little Dog Gone?

Materials: Dog Pattern (page 22), colorful paper, scissors, crayons or markers, hole punch, yarn

Make 22 enlarged copies of the Dog Pattern on colorful paper. Cut out the patterns, label them with two sets of numbers from 0 to 10. Laminate the cutouts for durability. Punch a hole at the top of each pattern and thread a piece of yarn through each one. Tie the ends of the yarn together to create necklaces. Give each student a necklace to wear. Have students scatter around the room and then look for classmates with matching numbers on their necklaces. When students find their matches, tell them to stand together until everyone has found a match.

Pet Shop

Materials: pet travel carriers, aquariums or large plastic tubs, empty cages, empty boxes; stuffed animals and plastic toys that represent various pets; food and water dishes; pet toys; collars and leashes; grooming supplies; first aid kit

Create a pet shop by placing the carriers, cages, and aquariums around the perimeter of a center. (If these are not available, use empty boxes turned on their sides.) Label the carriers with the types of animals that belong in them. Place the toy animals in the appropriate containers. Create a separate area for pet grooming and an area to serve as a veterinarian's office. Help students choose roles as employees or patrons of the pet shop. Encourage them to act out each role and then switch.

Good Dog!

Materials: Dog and Bone Patterns (page 23), scissors, glue, paper plates, brown paper, colorful markers, stickers

Make 10 enlarged copies of the Dog Pattern and cut them out. Glue the patterns to paper plates to make "dog dishes." Make 20 copies of the Bone Pattern on brown paper. On half of the bones, write numbers from 1 to 10. On the other half, write sets from 1 to 10. Code the backs of the matching bones with colorful stickers or markings for self-checking. Laminate the bones for durability. To play, have students spread the 10 dog dishes on the floor. Then, students should sort the dog bones so that each dog has a matching pair of bones. When they are finished, students can turn over all of the bones to check their work.

Five Speckled Frogs

Materials: Frog Patterns (page 24), green paper, card stock

Make a frog finger puppet for yourself and one for each student. Reduce and copy the Frog Patterns on green paper. Cut out the patterns and attach each to a ring of card stock that is sized to fit around the wearer's finger. Wear the finger puppets as you recite the following rhyme with students. The rhyme traditionally starts with five frogs; if desired, start the rhyme with 10 frogs.

Five Speckled Frogs

Five speckled frogs sitting on a log,	(hold up five fingers)
Eating some delicious bugs.	
Yum! Yum!	(pat stomach)
One frog jumped in the pool,	(hide puppet behind your back)
Where it was nice and cool,	
Now there are four speckled frogs.	(hold up four fingers)
Glub! Glub!	

Continue with "Four speckled frogs sitting on a log," etc., until there are no frogs left.

Taking Turns

Materials: Pet Cards (page 26)

Copy the Pet Cards. Cut out the animals in advance. Give each student an animal picture. Taking turns around the circle, have each student tell what animal she has, what she will name the pet, and one thing the pet does, eats, or likes.

Say Cheese!

Materials: yellow construction paper, black marker

Cut out 11 cheese wedge shapes from yellow paper. Using a black marker, draw a number of holes (circles) to make sets from 0 to 10 on each cheese wedge. Laminate the cheese wedges for durability. To play, have students count the number of holes on each cheese wedge and then place the patterns in order from the largest number of holes to the smallest number or from the smallest number to the largest number. Students can also randomly select two cheese wedge patterns and compare them to determine which has more holes and which has fewer holes.

Animal Riddles

Play this game like I Spy. Give hints about an animal while the class tries to guess what animal it is. For example, say "I am thinking of an animal that lives on a farm and gives milk. What is it?" (A cow). After demonstrating, let volunteers lead the game.

20

Who Has the Puppy?

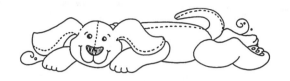

Materials: stuffed puppy or another stuffed animal

Have students sit in a circle with one student in the center. Tell the student in the center to close his eyes while the other students pass a stuffed puppy (or another animal) behind their backs. When the student in the center barks (or makes another animal signal), the student holding the stuffed animal must hold it still behind his back. The student in the center must stay seated, look around, and guess who has the puppy. Allow the student three guesses. If the student holding the puppy is not found, he moves to the center.

Bird, Bird, Cat

Have students sit in a circle. One student should be the bird who walks (flies) around the outside of the circle. The bird should say, "Bird," as it touches each student's head. Whenever the bird chooses, she should touch a student's head and say, "Cat." The cat must jump up and try to catch the bird. While running, the bird must say, "Tweet," while the cat says, "Meow." If the cat catches (tags) the bird, the bird moves to the center of the circle. If the bird runs all of the way around the circle without getting caught, she sits in the cat's place. The cat becomes the next bird. The next time a bird moves to the center, the first bird goes back to the circle.

Pet Transition

Dismiss students in groups by the types of pets that they have (or do not have) at home.

Birds on a Wire

Materials: Bird Pattern (page 25), colorful paper, yarn or string, clothespins or paper clips

Enlarge 11 copies of the Bird Pattern on colorful paper. On each bird, write a number from 0 to 10. Cut out the birds and laminate them for durability. Attach a piece of yarn or string across a bulletin board at students' eye level. Using clothespins or paper clips, have students attach the birds to the yarn in numerical order. For a challenge, have students arrange the birds in reverse numerical order.

Frog Patterns

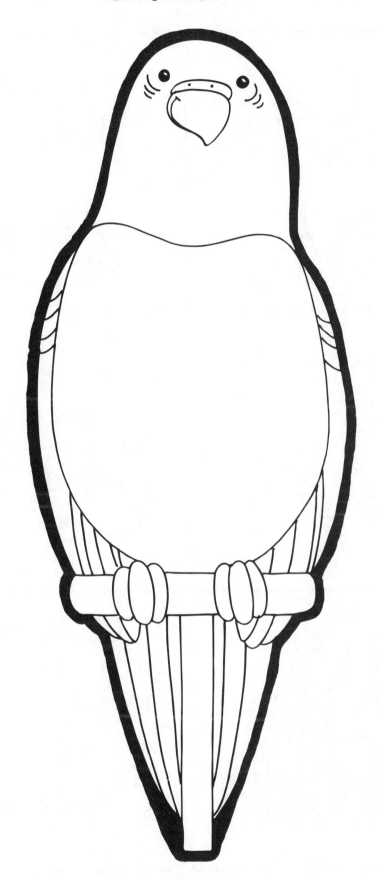

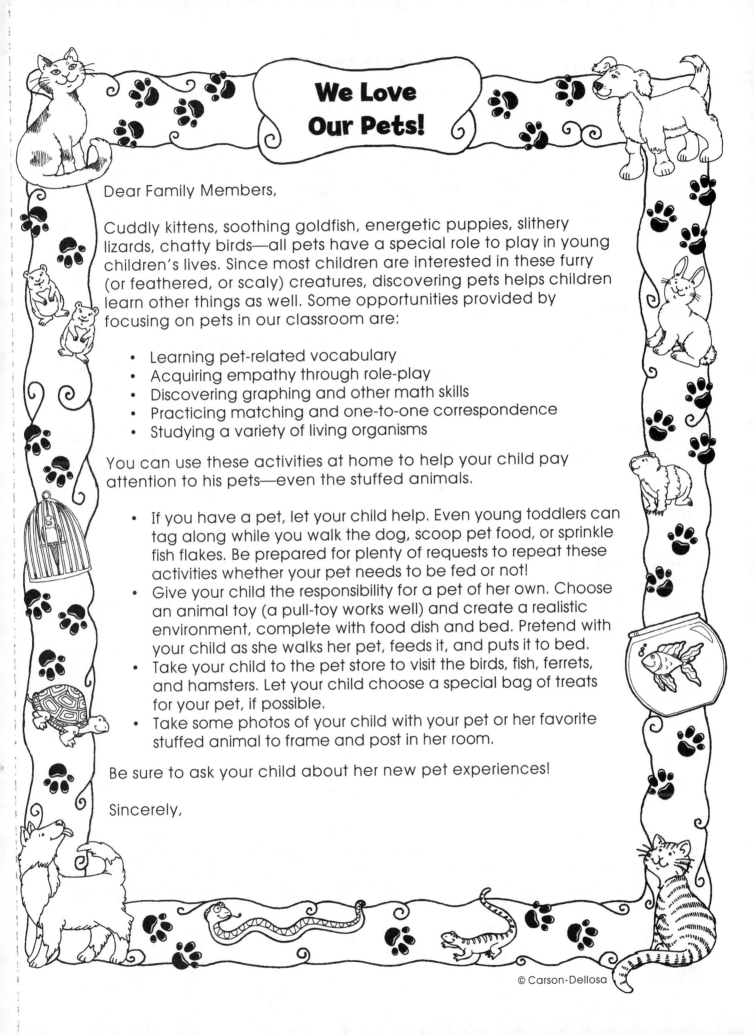

We Love Our Pets!

Dear Family Members,

Cuddly kittens, soothing goldfish, energetic puppies, slithery lizards, chatty birds—all pets have a special role to play in young children's lives. Since most children are interested in these furry (or feathered, or scaly) creatures, discovering pets helps children learn other things as well. Some opportunities provided by focusing on pets in our classroom are:

- Learning pet-related vocabulary
- Acquiring empathy through role-play
- Discovering graphing and other math skills
- Practicing matching and one-to-one correspondence
- Studying a variety of living organisms

You can use these activities at home to help your child pay attention to his pets—even the stuffed animals.

- If you have a pet, let your child help. Even young toddlers can tag along while you walk the dog, scoop pet food, or sprinkle fish flakes. Be prepared for plenty of requests to repeat these activities whether your pet needs to be fed or not!
- Give your child the responsibility for a pet of her own. Choose an animal toy (a pull-toy works well) and create a realistic environment, complete with food dish and bed. Pretend with your child as she walks her pet, feeds it, and puts it to bed.
- Take your child to the pet store to visit the birds, fish, ferrets, and hamsters. Let your child choose a special bag of treats for your pet, if possible.
- Take some photos of your child with your pet or her favorite stuffed animal to frame and post in her room.

Be sure to ask your child about her new pet experiences!

Sincerely,

A Trip to the Zoo

Going to the zoo is one of the most common excursions for students. Students love seeing in real life the animals they first get to know from books. What could be more exciting than seeing a polar bear swim, or hearing a lion roar, or watching a giant panda with its newborn close by? There is nothing like the appeal of zoo animals to teach more common preschool activities like counting, sequencing, and matching. But, teaching a zoo unit also presents a unique opportunity to teach about habitats, animal classification, and even animal behavior and movement. While books like *Good Night, Gorilla* provide humor, other selections like *Zoo-Looking* remind students of the role of zoos, and that animals inside should be treated with respect. The selections by Aliki and Fox would be especially helpful to read before a class trip to the zoo.

Literature Selections

Felicity Floo Visits the Zoo by E. S. Redmond (Candlewick Press, 2009). A clever account of Felicity's visit to the zoo. The message of the importance of using tissues and practicing proper hand washing to prevent germs from spreading is humorous yet clear.

Good Night, Gorilla by Peggy Rathmann (Putnam Juvenile, 1996). A sleepy night watchman wishes the zoo's gorilla a good night. But the gorilla—along with his parade of zoo animal friends tagging along behind him—thinks that they might be happier sleeping elsewhere.

My Visit to the Zoo by Aliki (HarperCollins, 1999). Beautiful, labeled pictures emphasize the beauty of a zoo and its role in conservation.

Zoo-Looking by Mem Fox (Mondo Publishing, 1996). Lest visitors forget that the animals in the zoo are alive and participating in the zoo experience, this colorful paper collage book showcases the animals looking back intently at one very excited visitor.

Zoo-ology by Joëlle Jolivet (Roaring Brook Press, 2003). A superbly drawn, life-size book introduces classification in terms that a student can understand, such as "Hot" and "Black and White."

Zoo Blocks

Materials: variety of blocks; small zoo animal figurines; small people figurines; vehicle toys, such as a train, a bus, and trucks

Encourage students to create a zoo using the blocks. Suggest building habitats, fences and walls, buildings, etc. Tell students that they can also use the zoo animals, people, and vehicles as part of the scene. Suggest using the bus to bring guests into the zoo, the train to ride around on a zoo tour, and the trucks for zookeepers to move from one animal habitat to another.

Animal Cracker Zoo

Materials: bowls (optional), food coloring (optional), graham crackers, cream cheese, animal crackers, plastic knives, disposable plates

If desired, separate the cream cheese into bowls and mix it with food coloring. Place the supplies on a table. Tell students that they will make animal habitats to build their own tasty zoos! The graham crackers will serve as the habitat areas for each type of animal. Explain the steps to students as you demonstrate the activity, then have each student make his own snack.

1. Have students break two graham crackers into two pieces so that they have four squares.
2. Let them spread cream cheese on the four pieces of cracker.
3. Allow students to choose one type of animal from the animal crackers and place some of that type on one graham cracker.
4. Repeat step 3 for the other pieces of graham cracker.
5. Students should arrange their four graham cracker habitats in a circle on their plate to make a zoo. Then, let them enjoy their snack!

 **(See page 2.)**

Animal Number Match

Materials: Zoo Animal Cards (pages 37–39), card stock, crayons or markers, scissors, resealable plastic bags

Make two copies of the Zoo Animal Cards on card stock. Color and cut apart the cards. On one set of cards, write numbers from 1 to 9. On the other set, draw sets of dots to represent numbers from 1 to 9. Do not write the matching numbers and sets of dots on the same animals. For example, if you write the number 2 on an elephant, draw the two dots on any animal except the other elephant. This will challenge students to match the numbers and dots rather than the types of animals. Laminate the cards for durability. Store each set of cards in a resealable plastic bag. Place the bags on a table in a math center. Have students remove the cards from the two bags. Tell them to place each set facedown on the table in a grid pattern. Then, let each student take turns flipping over one card from each set. If the numbers match, that student keeps the pair and takes another turn. If the numbers do not match, the student turns the two cards facedown and another student takes a turn. The game continues until all of the cards are matched.

Classifying Zoo Animals

Materials: paper, pencils and crayons, variety of zoo animals (stuffed or plastic figurines, or laminated pictures), 4 boxes or bins

Make four signs that say *mammal*, *bird*, *fish*, and *reptile*. Include illustrations of representative animals. Attach each sign to a box. Place the boxes on the floor and spread the animals in front of the boxes. Place the other supplies on a nearby table. Introduce students to the center by talking about the different kinds of animals that live in a zoo. Specifically mention these four categories and the characteristics that make these groups unique. Have students work together to sort the animals into the four boxes. Let them decide where each animal belongs and why. When students have finished sorting, have them draw pictures of the four groups of animals on a separate piece of paper.

Walk Like the Animals

Materials: Zoo Animal Cards (pages 37–39), scissors, crayons or markers

Enlarge the Zoo Animal Cards and cut them apart. Color and laminate them if desired. Have one student choose a card from the pile and secretly look at it. Have the student walk and act like that animal. (Depending on students' developmental levels, you may need to privately discuss the mannerisms of the selected animal with each student.) The rest of the class should try to guess which animal the student is imitating, and then have everyone join in to act like the animal. Repeat until everyone has had a turn or until all of the cards are gone.

Variation: Select a card from the stack. After noting the animal on the card, say, "If I were you, and I lived in the zoo . . . " Then, add a phrase that highlights a distinguishing characteristic of the animal you selected. If students cannot guess the animal from your first clue, continue adding clues until students can guess the animal that you are describing. Then, have students act like the chosen animal. Choose a new card and play again.

Monkeying Around

Materials: Monkey and Banana Patterns (page 34), brown paper, poster board, yellow paper, hook-and-loop tape

Make an enlarged copy of the Monkey Pattern on brown paper. Cut out and attach the monkey to a piece of poster board. Copy and cut out 22 banana shapes from yellow paper. On 11 bananas, write the numbers from 0 to 10. On the remaining 11 bananas, draw number sets from 0 to 10. Laminate the poster board and banana cutouts for durability. Attach hook-and-loop tape to the monkey's hands and to the backs of the bananas. To play, have one student choose a numbered banana and attach it to one of the monkey's hands. Then, have another student find the banana with the matching number set to place on the monkey's other hand. Play continues until all of the numbers and sets have been matched.

Lions and Tigers and Bears

Materials: a small stuffed lion, tiger, or bear; masking tape

Using tape, mark start and finish lines on opposite sides of the room. Have the class form a line on the start line. Choose a small stuffed lion, tiger, or bear. Have one student leave the room while another hides the animal. When the player who left the room returns, have the class quietly chant while tiptoeing one step at a time toward the finish line, "Lions and tigers and bears, oh my!" (Have students throw hands in the air when saying, "Oh my!") The chant should grow gradually louder as the student who is looking gets closer and closer to the hidden animal. When the animal is finally found, the other students should quickly run to the finish line and sit down. The last student to find a seat is "captured" by the animal and becomes the next student to search for the animal. If students reach the finish line before the animal is found, everyone returns to the beginning and the student who was looking chooses a new student to search for the animal.

Kangaroo Peekaboo

Materials: Kangaroo and Joey Patterns (page 35), light brown paper, scissors, crayons or markers

Make 11 copies of the Kangaroo and Joey Patterns on light brown paper. Cut out all of the kangaroos and joeys. On each kangaroo's pocket draw a number set from 0 to 10. Label each joey with a number from 0 to 10. Laminate all of the kangaroos and joeys for durability. Cut a slit along each kangaroo's pouch to create a pocket. Have students work in pairs to match the sets and numbers by sliding each joey into the correct kangaroo's pouch.

Zoo Rap

Say this rap with children and let them copy your motions.

Zoo Rap

I went to the zoo the other day, (hold right hand out to side)
And this is what the animals (hold left hand out to side)
Had to say . . . (put both hands to mouth)
The snakes said, "Hiss!" (move hand up and down in a wave across body)
The zebra said, "Eeep! Eeep!" (stomp one foot and toss head back)
The birds said, "Chirp!" (move index finger and thumb together in front of mouth)
And, "Eedle-deedle-deep." (flap arms and walk in a circle)
Zoo rap, zoo rap, eedle-deedle doo rap! (dance)
Zoo rap, zoo rap, eedle-deedle doo rap! (continue dancing)
I went to the zoo the other day, (hold right hand out to side)
And this is what the animals (hold left hand out to side)
Had to say . . . (put both hands to mouth)
The lion said, "Roar!" (place hands at the sides of face and toss head)
The monkey said, "Hoop!" (scratch under arm)
And the owl said, "Whoo?" (hold hands out, palms up and shrug shoulders)
And, "Hoodle-doodle-doo." (swing arms back and forth)
Zoo rap, zoo rap, hoodle-doodle-doo rap! (dance)
Zoo rap, zoo rap, hoodle-doodle-doo rap! (continue dancing)

Silly Snakes

Materials: permanent marker, two jump ropes

Using a permanent marker, draw snake facial features on one handle of each of the two jump ropes. Have students stand in a circle. Place the jump ropes on the floor in the middle of the circle. Ask students to take turns making "snake shapes" by manipulating the jump ropes to form circles, squares, rectangles, triangles, and other familiar shapes. When a student finishes forming a shape, have the other students identify the name of the shape. Then, let two students make shapes at the same time and have the other students compare the two shapes. Are they the same? If they are different, how? Are they the same size? Which shape has more angles?

Dressed-Up Bears

Materials: Bear and T-shirt Patterns (page 36), brown paper, colorful paper, crayons or markers, scissors

Make a class set of the Bear Pattern on brown paper. Label each bear with a number set. (If students only know numbers from 1 to 10 and there are more than 10 students in the class, make two sets of bears with numbers from 1 to 10.) Make a class set of the T-shirt Pattern on colorful paper and label each shirt with a number to match one of the bear patterns. Cut out the bears and T-shirts and laminate them for durability. During circle time, give each student a bear. Spread the shirts on the floor in the middle of the circle. Have each student take turns finding the T-shirts that match the sets on the bears.

Bear Laundry

Materials: large plastic basket (such as a laundry basket), hook-and-loop tape, Bear and T-shirt Patterns (page 36), brown paper, colorful paper, crayons or markers, scissors

Obtain a small plastic basket, such as a laundry basket. Attach a piece of hook-and-loop tape to the side of the basket. Make 10 copies of the Bear Pattern on brown paper. Label each bear with a number from 1 to 10. Make at least 10 copies of the T-shirt Pattern on colorful paper. Cut out the bears and T-shirts and laminate them for durability. Attach a piece of hook-and-loop tape to the back of each bear. To play the game, have a student attach a bear pattern to the laundry basket and then count and place the matching number of T-shirts inside the basket. Students can play this game with partners, as well.

turtle

owl

turkey

warthog

alligator

frog

flamingo

parrot

Zoo Animal Cards

tiger

peacock

snake

zebra

seal

duck

giraffe

chimpanzee

hippopotamus

lion

bear

elephant

walrus

kangaroo

gorilla

rhinoceros

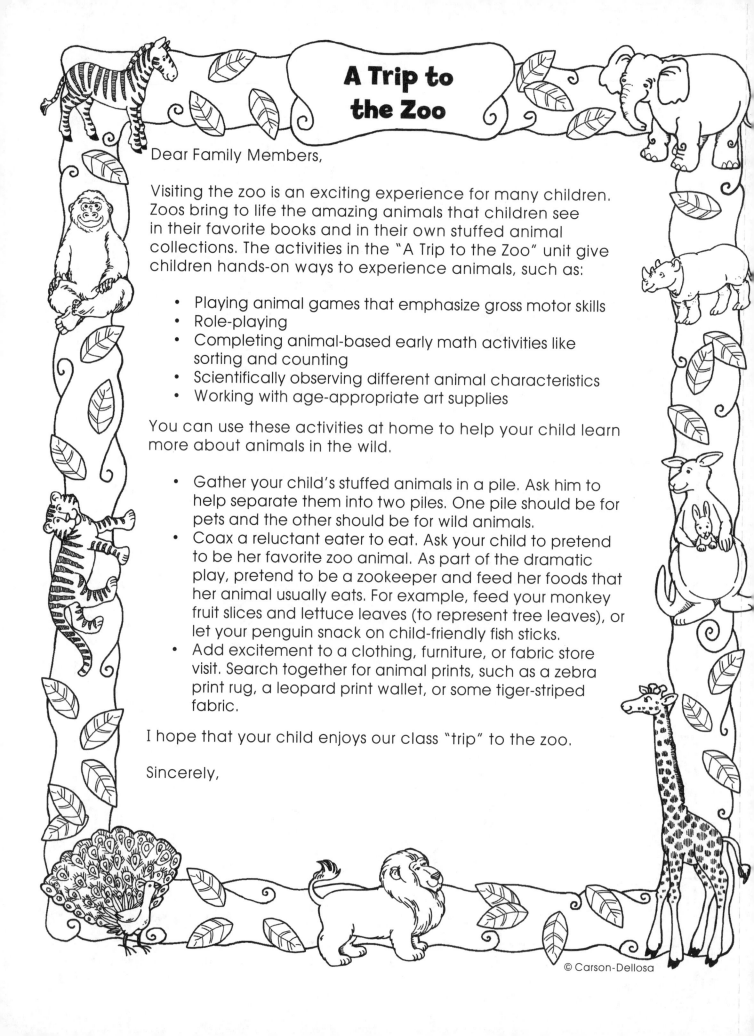

A Trip to the Zoo

Dear Family Members,

Visiting the zoo is an exciting experience for many children. Zoos bring to life the amazing animals that children see in their favorite books and in their own stuffed animal collections. The activities in the "A Trip to the Zoo" unit give children hands-on ways to experience animals, such as:

- Playing animal games that emphasize gross motor skills
- Role-playing
- Completing animal-based early math activities like sorting and counting
- Scientifically observing different animal characteristics
- Working with age-appropriate art supplies

You can use these activities at home to help your child learn more about animals in the wild.

- Gather your child's stuffed animals in a pile. Ask him to help separate them into two piles. One pile should be for pets and the other should be for wild animals.
- Coax a reluctant eater to eat. Ask your child to pretend to be her favorite zoo animal. As part of the dramatic play, pretend to be a zookeeper and feed her foods that her animal usually eats. For example, feed your monkey fruit slices and lettuce leaves (to represent tree leaves), or let your penguin snack on child-friendly fish sticks.
- Add excitement to a clothing, furniture, or fabric store visit. Search together for animal prints, such as a zebra print rug, a leopard print wallet, or some tiger-striped fabric.

I hope that your child enjoys our class "trip" to the zoo.

Sincerely,

Squishing through the mud, listening to the *rummm* of bullfrogs, tossing bread crumbs to see if fish come to the surface, looking out for turtles—these are just a few of the exciting adventures that happen when students visit ponds. Many students live in urban environments and do not have the opportunity to experience pond life, but this important habitat still captivates students, even when they are only able to imagine it in the classroom. Acquaint students with pond life through activities like butterfly art, discussions, pond animal riddles, and alligator games. Use *What's in the Pond?* and *Butternut Hollow Pond* to inspire more scientific investigations into pond life. After reading *Just a Day at the Pond*, discuss some topics that students would like to explore.

Literature Selections

Butternut Hollow Pond by Brian J. Heinz (First Avenue Editions, 2005). Everybody at the pond is hungry, it seems. This book touches on the science of the food chain as it describes what pond creatures need for survival.

Foo, the Flying Frog of Washtub Pond by Belle Yang (Candlewick Press, 2009). On the banks of Washtub Pond, Foo Frog grows larger than friends Sue-Lin Salamander and Mao-Mao Mudpuppy. As Foo Frog grows, so does his ego. Some foolish adventures teach him some great lessons.

In the Small, Small Pond by Denise Fleming (Henry Holt and Co. BYR Paperbacks, 2007). Fleming's paper collages and on-target text capture the essence of pond animals. This book also demonstrates how the seasons change.

Just a Day at the Pond by Mercer Mayer (HarperFestival, 2008). Little Critter knows how to swim—sort of. Students will identify with his reluctance to get into the pond as they enjoy the creatures that he encounters.

What's in the Pond? (Hidden Life) by Anne Hunter (Sandpiper, 1999). Appealing, realistic illustrations help students learn to identify pond creatures.

Butterfly Matching

Materials: Butterfly Pattern (page 44), scissors, wallpaper samples, construction paper, sandpaper, other textured paper

Use the Butterfly Pattern to cut butterfly shapes. Trace two patterns on wallpaper samples, construction paper, sandpaper, and other textured papers. Cut out two butterflies from each color or pattern. Allow each student to take turns matching the butterflies.

Pond Life

Materials: pictures of a pond

Talk about what animals live around a pond, such as ducks, beavers, frogs, salamanders, snakes, turtles, red-winged blackbirds, insects, spiders, butterflies, and so on. Look at pictures of a pond and describe the plants that grow there. Talk about the sounds that you might hear around a pond. Listen to each student's story about visiting a pond. Teach students respect for living things by explaining the proper way to treat plants and animals that live at a pond.

Extension: Many students think that a frog says, "ribbit." Find audio samples of different frog sounds by downloading frog calls from the Internet.

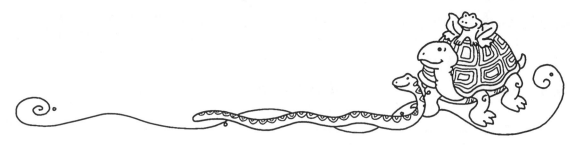

Frogs and Alligators

Materials: green construction paper, scissors, tape

Alligators are known for their speed and their powerful jaws. To be successful in this game, the "frogs" must get all of the way around the room without getting caught by the "alligator" that is waiting just under the water. Cut out several lily pads of various sizes from large, green construction paper. Tape them to the floor in a big circle, about 18" (46 cm) apart, so that they are close enough to step across, but far enough apart that each student has to stretch a little to reach the next lily pad. Choose one student to be the alligator that is waiting in the middle of the pond.

Have the frogs take turns moving from one lily pad to the next around the circle. If a frog steps off of a lily pad into the "water," the alligator must be alert enough to see it happen and call out the frog's name. If the alligator is successful in "catching" a frog in the water, the frog becomes the next alligator. When the frogs seem to have mastered their trip around the lily pads, have them move faster and faster or try various ways of getting from one lily pad to the next, such as hopping on one foot or leapfrogging.

Pond Riddles

Tell students that you are thinking of a plant or animal that grows or lives at the pond. Tell them one attribute of the plant or animal. Allow them to question you about the plant or animal, then to try to guess what it is. Select students to choose a plant or animal for others to guess.

Swan Song

This is a Mother Goose rhyme with a finger play. Have students stand so that they can swim away and back.

Swan Song

Swan swam over the sea,	(make swan's head; move forward)
Swim, swan, swim!	(dog paddle)
Swan swam back again,	(make swan's head; move backward)
Well swum, swan!	(clap for swan)

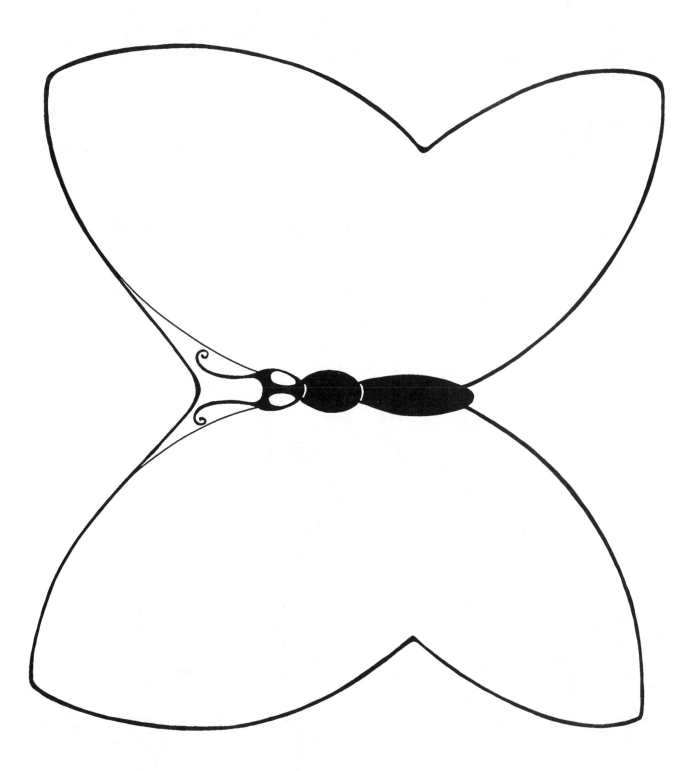

Life at the Pond

Dear Family Members,

Most children are fascinated by ponds. Discoveries are unlimited near a pond, and they all involve mud, water, and unique plants and animals. These pond-related activities give children many opportunities, such as:

- Exploring a natural environment
- Playing pond games to use gross motor skills
- Formulating and responding to questions
- Working with art supplies to use fine motor skills

You can use these activities at home to help your child learn more about pond life.

- Create your own bathtub "pond." Toss a few plastic pond animals and green and blue, bathtub-safe coloring tablets into the tub and let your child dive in. For extra fun, let your child wear goggles and look under the water.
- Some snakes swim in ponds. How do snakes move through water? Let your child take a piece of rope into the bathtub. Teach her to pull the rope as she moves her hand from side to side. Explain that snakes move through water by moving their bodies the same way.
- If you live near a pond, observe it close-up. Scoop a jar of pond water, cover it, and let your child observe what is in the water. Ask questions like, "Is it clear or cloudy?" or "What is floating in the water?" Look for animals in the jar.
- Describe a beaver dam to your child, then build one. Push two pieces of furniture close together, and let your child block the opening with pillows. Pretend to be the "water" crashing through the "dam."

Have fun with your pond adventures!

Sincerely,

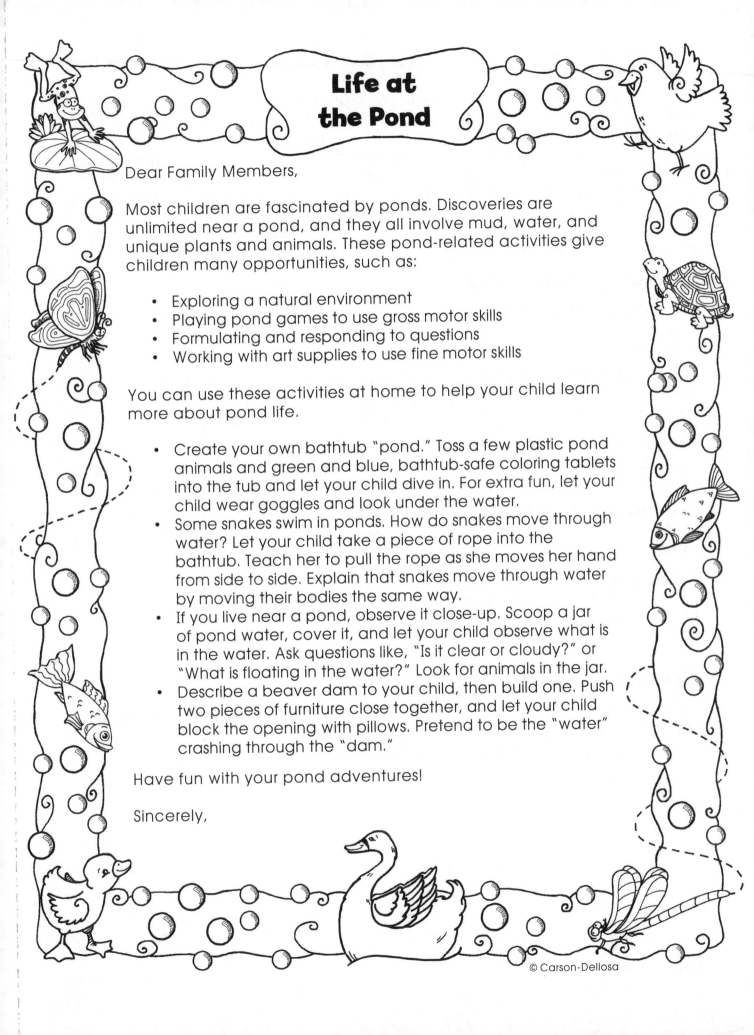

Whether you introduce this theme during a summer program, just before school lets out for summer, or in the middle of winter, students are sure to find a unit about the ocean and the beach very appealing. The prospect of a giant sand-and-water table coupled with interesting sea animals make learning about the beach a delightful vacation for students. Use ocean animals to inspire activities like an octopus snack, ocean animal rhymes and finger plays, classification and sorting, beach ball language experiences, and sandy art projects. Read *I'm the Biggest Thing in the Ocean* when you measure students' heights, or combine *Into the A, B, Sea: An Ocean Alphabet Book* with letter recognition activities.

Literature Selections

A House for Hermit Crab by Eric Carle (Aladdin, 2005). In addition to learning about hermit crabs, students will also learn about the calendar, friendship, and how to turn a house into a home.

All the World by Liz Garton Scanlon (Beach Lane Books, 2009). A child's connection to nature and to the world of human beings is beautifully illustrated. People of various cultures are featured working and playing together.

I'm the Biggest Thing in the Ocean by Kevin Sherry (Dial, 2007). In this hilarious book, an extremely confident squid compares his size favorably to everything he sees (even the book's barcode), even after he gets swallowed by a bigger whale.

Into the A, B, Sea: An Ocean Alphabet Book by Deborah Lee Rose (Scholastic, 2000). Rhyming couplets and vivid illustrations of unique sea creatures teach students about fascinating animals.

Swimmy by Leo Lionni (Dragonfly Books, 1973). Lionni's subtle aquatic tale about diversity and forming alliances shows small fish working together to defeat the bigger, hungry fish in the sea.

She Sells Seashells

Say this as a call-and-response tongue twister. One group or individual should say the first line and a second group or individual should say the second line. Students will have fun taking turns saying the different lines.

She sells seashells by the seashore.

Seashells for sale! Seven cents a shell!

Octopus Pears

Materials: canned pear halves, disposable plates, plastic knives, chocolate chips

Open the canned pears. Place all of the supplies on a table. Explain the steps to students as you demonstrate the activity. Each student should then follow the recipe.

1. Have each student place a pear half flat side down on a plate.
2. Help each student cut seven slits in the wide part of the pear.
3. Each student should poke the points of two chocolate chips into the top of her pear for eyes.
4. Help students count the octopus's legs before enjoying their snacks!

 **(See page 2.)**

Five Little Crabs

Have students count on their fingers as you lead them in this chant.

Five Little Crabs

Five little crabs playing on the shore.
One skittered off and then there were four.
Four little crabs feeling rather free.
One saw a snack and then there were three.
Three little crabs wondered what to do.
One caught a wave and then there were two.
Two little crabs basking in the sun.
One got too hot and then there was one.
One little crab feeling all alone,
Slipped in the water and all the crabs were home.

Sorting Sea Life

Materials: Ocean Animal Patterns (pages 50–51), colorful paper, scissors

Copy two sets of the Ocean Animal Patterns on colorful paper. Repeat the process with a reduced set of copies and an enlarged set of copies. Cut out the animals and laminate them for durability. Have students sort the animals by species, color, or size. If desired, challenge students to time themselves to see how quickly they can sort the cutouts. Then, let them try to beat their own best times. The cutouts can also be used for patterning activities.

Beach Ball Colors

Materials: striped beach ball with traditional colors

Have students stand in a large circle. Say a student's name as you toss the beach ball and say, "Left thumb!" or "Right thumb!" while the ball is still in the air. The student should catch the ball and say the name of the color that the thumb is touching. She must then toss the ball, say another student's name, and say, "Left thumb!" or "Right thumb!"

Counting Ocean Animals Mini-Book

Materials: Counting Animals Mini-Book (page 49), scissors, stapler, pencils, crayons or markers

Help students create counting mini-books. Make an enlarged copy of the Counting Animals Mini-Book for each student. Then, cut along the dotted lines and staple the pages together to make mini-books. Give each student a mini-book and let her write her name on the cover. Encourage students to color the animals after they count them aloud. Let students take the completed books home to continue counting practice. (If students are able to write numbers from 1 to 5, cover the numbers on the mini-book page before making copies. Then, students can write the numbers themselves when they count the animals.)

2 turtles

5 starfish

1 octopus

4 fish

I Can Count to 5!

Name: _____

3 dolphins

Ocean in Motion

Dear Family Members,

Ahoy, families! We are hitting the beach in our classroom and surrounding ourselves with sand, surf, shells, and sea creatures. As children soak up the rays, they are experiencing some surfer-ific ocean activities, such as:

- Working with books and prereading
- Counting and patterning
- Taking a pretend "field trip" to the beach
- Learning new gross motor movements
- Learning mathematical concepts like *more/less* and *big/small*

Try some of these at-home activities to help your child learn more about life near the shore.

- If you have any pinch clothespins or chip bag binders, let your child hold one in each hand and pretend to be a crab. Let him perform simple tasks like color, put away toys, and even eat a snack while using his "claws" for hands.
- Share some easy, beachy snacks like fish-shaped and starfish-shaped crackers or gummy fish fruit snacks.
- Try a science experiment. Let your child choose waterproof toys to drop in the bathtub. Predict whether they will sink or float.
- Make a "clam" sandwich. Spread some mayonnaise on a flour tortilla. Add one slice of lunch meat and some shredded cheese, then fold the tortilla in half. Lightly toast the sandwich to melt the cheese. Before serving, peel open the sandwich a little and add olive "eyes" (or carrot circles) that peek at your child. Place the sandwich on a bed of "seaweed" (shredded lettuce).

Have a fun beach trip at home with your child.

Sincerely,

Birds, Birds, Birds

It is hard not to notice birds, especially when they are singing. Young students often delight in hearing birds, watching them eat and feed their chicks, finding birds' nests, and seeing flocks of them take flight. Highlight the birds around you by leading students to observe where they live, what they look like, and what they eat. Help enhance students' fine motor skills by letting them pretend to feed baby birds, improve their measuring skills by letting them measure bird seed, and sharpen their observational skills by taking them on an outdoor birding adventure. *Birds, Nests and Eggs* offers a scientific approach to studying birds, while the other stories celebrate their entertainment value. Read *Tacky the Penguin* to celebrate our flightless bird friends, and gently explore a birds' place in the food chain with *Feathers for Lunch*.

Literature Selections

Birds, Nests and Eggs by Mel Boring (NorthWord Books for Young Readers, 1998). This beautifully illustrated guide to birding depicts 15 birds and their chicks, habitats, and nests.

Boo Hoo Bird by Jeremy Tankard (Scholastic, 2009). Not every day is a good day, but the distraction of friends can often be the best medicine. *Boo Hoo Bird* is a great book after an attack of the boo hoos.

Feathers for Lunch by Lois Ehlert (Sandpiper, 1996). When a cat wants to add wild birds to his diet, he is rewarded with nothing but feathers. Bold paper illustrations make the birds in this book easily recognizable.

Little Bird, Biddle Bird by David Kirk (Scholastic, 2001). The mother bird watches proudly as her youngster forages for food all by himself.

Tacky the Penguin by Helen Lester (Houghton Mifflin, 1990). Tacky marches to the beat of a different drummer, but his fellow penguins learn to appreciate him when he saves them from a pack of hunters.

Jelly Bean Count

Materials: index cards cut into fourths, large basket of plastic eggs, jelly beans, bowl, paper cups

Write a number from 1 to 5 on each piece of index card. Put one numbered piece of index card inside each plastic egg. Put all of the eggs in the basket, pour the jelly beans into the bowl, and give each student a paper cup. Place all of the supplies on a table in a center. Have each student select five eggs from the basket. Tell them to open the eggs one at a time and read the numbers on the cards. For each number, students should place that number of jelly beans in their cups. After they have opened the five eggs and put the jelly beans into their cups, have them remove all of the jelly beans from their cups and count them to find the total.

Feeding the Birds

Materials: Baby Bird Patterns (page 57), crayons or markers, scissors, small paper cups, bowl of uncooked elbow macaroni, tweezers

Copy, color, and cut out the Baby Bird Patterns. Glue a Baby Bird Pattern to each paper cup. Place all of the supplies on a table. Tell students to pretend that they are adult birds and that the small paper cups are baby birds. Explain that the tweezers represent bird beaks and the macaroni represents little worms. Have students use the tweezers to "feed" the "baby birds" by transferring pieces of macaroni, one at a time, from the bowl to the baby bird cups. Encourage students to feed the baby birds as much as possible, counting the "worms" aloud as they drop them into the baby bird cups.

Feather Painting

Materials: bowls; tempera paint; variety of feathers, both soft and stiff (available at craft stores); paper

Place the supplies on a table in a center. Have each student paint on his paper using feathers. Let him experiment with the different types of feathers using a variety of techniques. For example, he can try printing (pressing paint-dipped feathers onto the paper) or brushing and dabbing with the feathers.

Bird-watching

Materials: photographs of birds from magazines, child-sized binoculars, paper, pencils and crayons

Display the bird photographs on the wall. Place the supplies on a table near the photographs. Tell students to observe the bird photographs with and without the binoculars. Encourage them to study each bird and to try to name three things that are interesting or different about each bird. On sheets of paper, have students draw pictures of their favorite birds and write or dictate interesting characteristics that they noticed.

Extension: Place a bird feeder outside a classroom window. Let students use the binoculars to study the birds that visit the feeder. Have students draw pictures and write or dictate stories about the birds they observe.

Counting Feathers

Materials: play dough, Bird Head Pattern (page 57), card stock, number cards, feathers (available at craft stores)

Make a bird body using play dough (a round ball shape). Make a copy of the Bird Head Pattern on card stock and cut it out. Push the paper bird head into one side of the bird body. Show a number card and have students take turns putting the correct number of tail feathers into the bird body. Have students count feathers and push them into the opposite side of the bird body to form a tail. To involve more students, prepare three birds using play dough, and let three students at a time count and add feathers. Compare the number of feathers in each. Then, choose a different number and have three other students count feathers. To make this a center activity, duplicate several bird heads on different colors of construction paper and write the numerals on the bird heads. Students can change the heads and numbers of feathers to make different birds.

Finch, Finch, Blue Jay

Blue jays are aggressive birds at the feeder. When they arrive, the other birds seem to scatter. Have students sit in a circle, forming a "bird feeder." Designate one student to be "it." She should walk around the outside of the circle. She may gently tap two students on the head and say, "Finch." Those finches should stand in the center of the circle and wait until the person who is "it" chooses the blue jay. When the blue jay is tapped on the head, she should stand up and try to shoo away the finches. The finches must run around the inside of the circle and try to sit down in an empty spot before the blue jay can tag them. Whoever is tagged is the next "it." If no one is tagged, the blue jay becomes "it."

Bird Sounds

Materials: pictures of various birds (optional)

Children are already familiar with many bird sounds, such as the quack of a duck, and probably the sounds of some regional backyard birds. You can name a bird (or display a picture) and ask the students to make the bird sound, or you can make the sounds and ask the students to name (or point to) the birds. Make up a sound pattern using bird calls. For example, "hoot, quack, quack, hoot." Repeat the pattern a few times, and then have the students join you.

Feathers

Materials: variety of feathers in different sizes, textures, and colors (available at most craft stores); sensory table

Place the feathers in the sensory table. Encourage students to place their hands into the feathers. Tell them to look carefully at the different kinds of feathers and talk to each other about the similarities and differences they notice.

 **(See page 2.)**

Measuring Seed

Materials: large bowl of bird seed; measuring cups and spoons; assortment of containers in various sizes; sensory table or large, shallow box (optional)

Fill the large bowl halfway with bird seed. Place the supplies on a table. (For easy cleanup, place the supplies in a sensory table or large, shallow box.) Have students use the measuring cups and spoons to measure the seed from the large bowl into the other various containers. Ask them to find out how many cups or spoonfuls are needed to fill each container. Also, have them determine how the cups relate to each other—how many 1/4 cups are needed to fill 1/2 cup, how many 1/3 cups are needed to fill 1 cup, etc.

Seed Shakers

Materials: bowls containing different sizes of seeds, such as corn, beans, and bird seed; two small containers with lids for each student

As you pour each seed type into a bowl, explain that birds eat many kinds of seeds. Place the supplies on a table. Keep the empty seed containers beside the corresponding bowls so that students can identify each type of seed. Give each student two containers with lids. Next, have each student choose two different kinds of seeds. He should pinch a small amount of each, and place them in his two separate containers. Help him tightly close the containers. Then, tell students to shake their containers to hear the differences in the sounds.

Extension: Prepare two opaque containers of each type of seed. Close the containers and place them on a table. Encourage students to try to match the containers by listening to the sounds they make when they are shaken.

Birds, Birds, Birds

Dear Family Members,

Lately, our classroom is for the birds! Your children are learning a lot about our fine-feathered friends with activities from our "Birds, Birds, Birds" unit. Children are having fun:

- Working on unusual fine motor and sensory activities
- Working with manipulatives
- Making scientific observations
- Creating two- and three-dimensional art
- Learning mathematical concepts like *standard and nonstandard measurement* and *counting*

Let your child spread her wings at home with these fun activities.

- It is easy to pretend to be a bird. Let your child "perch" in a laundry basket lined with a sheet or blanket. Add plastic balls for eggs. Then, hide gummy worm fruit snacks on tables or chairs for your little bird to find and eat.
- Make "wings" for your child. Flatten two shoeboxes or cut apart the longer sides of a larger box. Place them on top of his arms and use masking tape underneath to attach them. As your child flaps his "wings," ask if he can feel the wind pushing up against them.
- If you have binoculars, let your child watch birds. Or, simply sit outside and listen together to the different bird songs.
- Explain that hummingbirds eat small insects and drink sweet flower nectar. Give your child a straw and a small cup of red fruit juice (or water with a few drops of red food coloring added). Let your child drink through the straw just like a hummingbird.

We hope you are looking forward to a whole flock of fun!

Sincerely,

Bugs do not always inspire the best of feelings, but they are fascinating creatures, and very important ones too. They are a food source for other animals, they pollinate flowers, and sometimes they even eat other insects, helping to control the pest population. Open students' eyes to the insect world with these buggy activities that will also help them learn to count, acquire new buggy vocabulary, and try some new art projects, like Butterfly Patterns. Use the literature selections below to highlight cockroaches, butterflies, spiders, flies, and a familiar, favorite caterpillar that just cannot seem to get enough to eat.

Literature Selections

Crickwing by Janell Cannon (Sandpiper, 2005). Crickwing is a cockroach who tires of being bullied by larger animals, and so decides to bully some leaf cutter ants. Their change of heart toward him leads Crickwing to a great act of kindness. Interesting insect facts are included in the back of the book.

The Icky Bug Counting Book by Jerry Pallotta (Charlesbridge Publishing, 1992). Add a fun spin on counting with creepy crawly bugs.

Miss Spider's Tea Party by David Kirk (Scholastic, 2007). Miss Spider just wants to invite a few friends for a tea party, but she has a hard time convincing them that she only eats flowers.

The Very Hungry Caterpillar by Eric Carle (Philomel, 1981). This children's classic has a very simple story line and a richly satisfying ending.

The Very Ugly Bug by Liz Pichon (Tiger Tales, 2007). "Be happy with who you are" is the constant message of this cute story. The witty text and colorful artwork highlight this story about self-acceptance.

Spiderweb Maze

Materials: black yarn, tape

Create your own spiderweb by crisscrossing black yarn back and forth on the floor. Secure the yarn with a piece of tape before changing directions. Ask students to maneuver through the spiderweb without touching any of the yarn.

Extension: Make the web maze more challenging by adding another dimension. Instead of making a flat web on the floor, pass the yarn over desks and around chair legs and other obstacles so that students have to step over or crawl through the web without getting caught.

A Colony of Ants

Materials: two or three beanbags for each student, a box

Explain that ants work together for the well-being of all of the ants in the colony. Each ant has a specific job, such as gathering food or building bridges. Ants use their sense of smell to follow the scent of the ants in front of them and to know where to find food.

Collect two or three beanbags for each student. Place the beanbags in a box on one side of the room. Have all of the little "ants" form a single line. Remind them that they should follow the path that the first little ant travels in order to find "food." Have the first ant in line crawl quickly across the room, choosing her path as she goes. The rest of the ants should follow closely behind her. When they arrive at the box of beanbags, each ant should grab one, balance it on his back, and continue following the leader back to the anthill. The second time, have another ant lead the group, creating a different trail for the others to follow.

Busy Bees

Like ants, bumblebees are very busy little creatures. They also have a way of defending themselves. If someone bothers a bumblebee, that person is likely to be stung. Have one student be the "bumblebee." At your signal, have students dart around the play area trying not to get "stung" by the bumblebee. When the bumblebee catches another player, he tags her, and that student must sit to the side of the play area to await the next game. The last student standing is the next bumblebee. Continue playing until everyone has had a chance to be the bumblebee. For a fast-paced game, have two or more students be bumblebees.

Insect Patterns

Materials: Insect Patterns (page 67), scissors, glue, large paper

Make at least four copies of the Insect Patterns and cut them apart. Glue the insects on large paper so that they are easy to hold. Have four to six students stand where everyone can see them. Give them insect cards to hold in a simple pattern, such as "ant, beetle, butterfly; ant, beetle, butterfly." Ask volunteers to determine the next insect in the pattern. Repeat until everyone can identify the pattern.

A "Lady" Bug?

Say this rhyme with students and discuss whether they think that all ladybugs are ladies.

Ladybugs

Although we call them "Ladybugs,"
Some ladybugs are men!
So why don't we call them "Gentlemen Bugs,"
Every now and then?

Going Buggy!

Materials: bug stamps or stickers, sentence strips

Using bug stamps or stickers, create several simple patterns on sentence strips. Have students select a sentence strip and use additional stamps or stickers to continue the pattern. Provide extra stamps or stickers and sentence strips for students to make their own patterns.

Alphabet Picnic

Materials: insect guide

Tell students that they are pretending to go on a picnic. Have students sit in a circle and take turns thinking of bugs that they will see on their picnic. They must think of insects that begin with the letters of the alphabet in order. Each student should say, "We're going on a picnic and I will see a(n) _____." For example, the first student might say, "We're going on a picnic and I will see an ant." The second student may say, "We're going on a picnic and I will see a beetle." Continue around the circle. If someone cannot think of an insect, the other students may help or you may consult an insect guide. To make the game more challenging, have students remember all of the insects that came before them in order: "We're going on a picnic and I will see an ant, a beetle, and a cockroach."

Spiders and Insects

Say this rhyme with students as you perform the motions.

Spiders and Insects

Spiders have eight legs.   (wiggle four fingers on each hand)

Insects have six.   (wiggle three fingers on each hand)

Insects have two wings   (spread arms as wings)

To fly away, quick!   (flap arms)

Black and Yellow Bees

Materials: Bee Patterns (page 68), scissors

Copy and cut out the Bee Patterns. Have students use the bees as counting tools as the rhyme is said. This counting rhyme can be adapted for practicing tens by starting with fifty bees and having ten take a dive.

Black and Yellow Bees

Five black and yellow bees
Finding nectar in flowers and trees.
One took a dive into the hive.
Now there are four searching bees.

Four black and yellow bees
Finding nectar in flowers and trees.
One took a dive into the hive.
Now there are three searching bees.

Three black and yellow bees
Finding nectar in flowers and trees.
One took a dive into the hive.
Now there are two searching bees.

Two black and yellow bees
Finding nectar in flowers and trees.
One took a dive into the hive.
Now there is one searching bee.

One black and yellow bee
Finding nectar in flowers and trees.
He took a dive into the hive.
Now there are no more searching bees.

Butterfly Patterns

Materials: Butterfly Pattern (page 69), dot stickers

Make one copy of the Butterfly Pattern for each student. Give each student a pattern and a supply of colorful dot stickers. On one butterfly wing, have students create a simple pattern using the dot stickers. If necessary, provide parameters, such as how many stickers and how many different colors can be used. Then, have each student exchange his butterfly with a classmate. Let each student use the dot stickers to duplicate the pattern on the butterfly's other wing.

Caterpillar Snacks

Materials: *The Very Hungry Caterpillar* by Eric Carle (Philomel, 1981), bulletin board paper, crayons or markers, a small paper square for each student

Read *The Very Hungry Caterpillar* by Eric Carle aloud to students and then use the story to create a pictograph. Draw a grid with five columns on a large piece of bulletin board paper. Label each column with the name and a picture of each type of fruit that the caterpillar eats in the story (apple, pear, plum, strawberry, watermelon, and orange). Read the story aloud a second time and have students take turns coloring a square on the graph for each piece of fruit that the caterpillar eats. When the graph is finished, have students count aloud how many pieces of fruit the caterpillar ate. Ask questions about the graph that challenge students to judge amounts like more, less, most, least, etc. Extend the activity by creating a second graph labeled with the same fruits. Give each student a paper square and tell her to write her name on it. When called upon, have each student place her square on the graph to indicate which fruit is her favorite.

Count the Spots

Materials: Ladybug Pattern (page 66), red paper, milk caps, black paint (or black construction paper)

Students can work independently or in pairs to complete this activity. Make 11 copies of the Ladybug Pattern on red paper. Label each pattern with a number from 0 to 10. Laminate the ladybugs for durability. To make counters, paint 55 milk caps with black paint. Or, cut out 55 circles from black construction paper and laminate for durability.
To play the game, have a student read the number on a ladybug and use the counters to place the matching number of spots on the ladybug's back.

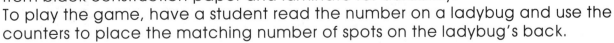

The Eency Weency Spider

You can add your own verses to this fun rhyme. Where might the spider try to climb at school?

The Eency Weency Spider

The eency weency spider went up the waterspout.
(put index fingers to thumbs alternately to make a climbing motion)

Down came the rain and washed the spider out.
(wiggle ten fingers down from the "sky" and move open hands to each side)

Out came the sun and dried up all the rain.
(arms in circle overhead)

And the eency weency spider went up the spout again.
(fingers climb again)

The eency weency spider went up the kitchen chair.
(fingers climb up)

Down came a foot and knocked it out of there.
(bring foot down)

Dinnertime was done and all the chairs pushed in.
(wipe hands together and push an imaginary chair in)

And the eency weency spider climbed up with a big grin.
(fingers climb up, then fingers at corners of smile)

The eency weency spider crawled up the bedroom door.
(fingers climb up)

On went the light and scared him to the floor.
(hands flash open on both sides of head)

When a window opened, he scurried to get out.
(fingers quickly move up)

And the eency weency spider went back to that waterspout!
(hands open out, palms up)

Shoo Fly

Sing this song and do the motions with students.

Shoo Fly

Shoo fly, don't bother me.
(wiggle fingers, then push away with hand)

Shoo fly, don't bother me.
(repeat motions)

Shoo fly, don't bother me.
(repeat motions)

I belong to somebody.
(point to self; hug self)

Busy Bugs

Materials: fast- and slow-paced music

Have students pretend to be bugs that you name. Play fast-paced music for flies, bees, dragonflies, and mosquitoes. Play slow-paced music for praying mantises, grasshoppers, and ladybugs. Give students a chance to name insects too. Explain that they may add sound effects, but make sure that children know not to "sting" or "bite."

Web Weaving

Materials: scissors, disposable plates, colorful yarn, tape

Use scissors to cut 1" (2.5 cm) slits, spaced approximately 2" (5 cm) apart, around the perimeter of each disposable plate. Cut the yarn into pieces, each approximately 1 yd. (1 m) in length. Place all of the supplies on a table. Have each student select a plate, then choose a piece of yarn and tape one end to the back of his plate. Then, tell him to weave the yarn in a random pattern by wrapping it around the plate and through the precut slits. When he reaches the end of a piece of yarn, have him tape the end to the back of the plate and select another piece of yarn. Let him continue until he has created a yarn web on his plate.

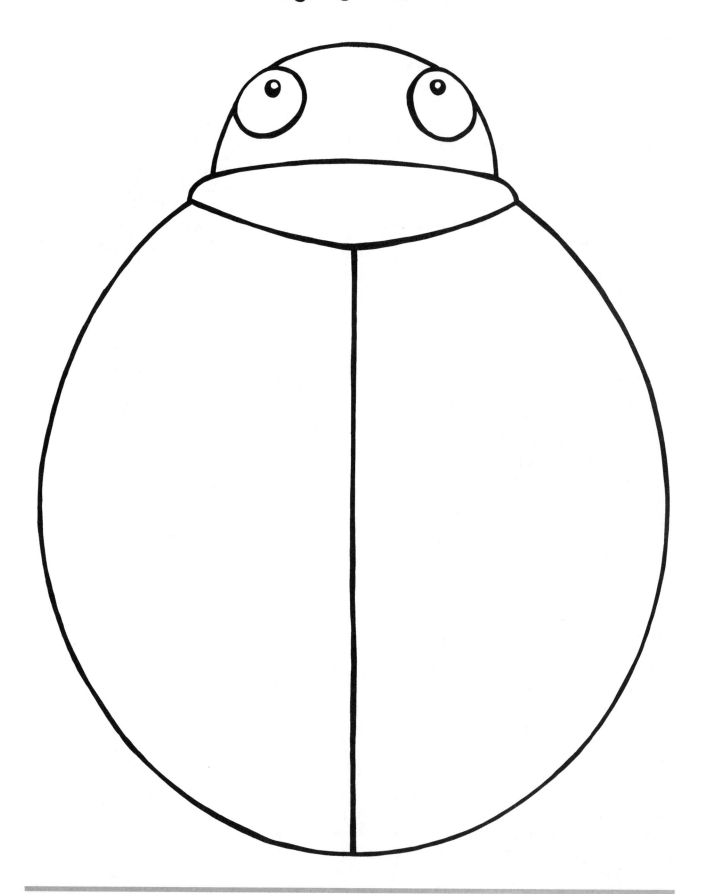

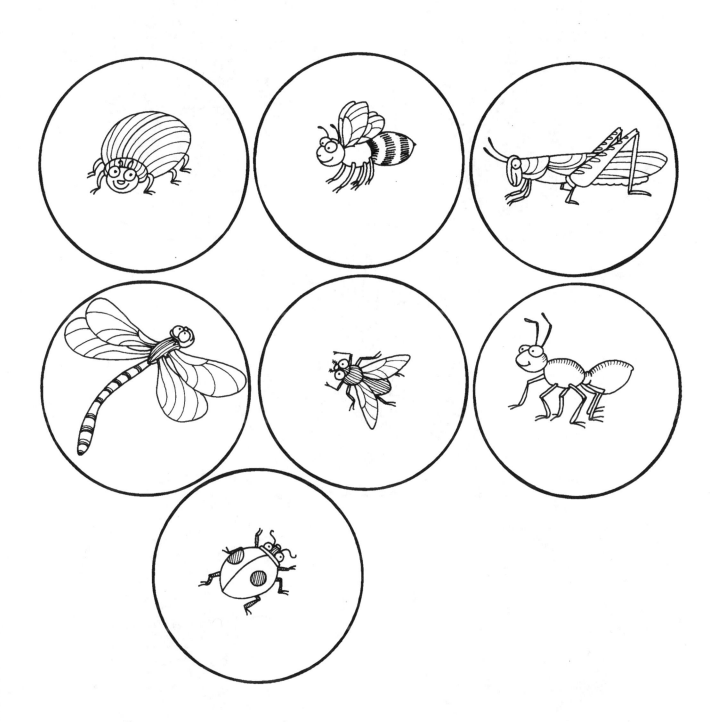

Bugs, Bugs, Bugs

Dear Family Members,

Crawly bugs are fun to watch—and they are a little creepy too. In the classroom, children are learning about our six-legged (and eight-legged) friends as they complete spider and insect games, activities, and artwork. "Everybuggy" is having fun with:

- Buggy rhymes and finger plays
- Counting forward and backward
- Discussing their feelings (positive and negative) about bugs
- Playing cooperative games
- Learning one-to-one correspondence

Your child will be buzzing with excitement during these spider and insect-themed activities that can be done at home.

- Find a spider that is building its web. Sit together and watch it weave the web. Then, watch to see if any bugs get caught in it.
- Give your child a ball of yarn or spool of string and let her weave her own spiderweb by winding it over furniture and around doorknobs. Be sure to remove any breakables.
- Look for bugs outdoors with a magnifying glass. Make sure that you lift rocks or logs to get a closer look at the bugs hiding underneath.
- If your child is over age one, let her taste some honey. Drizzle it on some bread and talk about how bees make it.
- Practice bug kindness in your house. The next time you or your child find a bug inside, let it outside instead of ending its life.

We hope you are looking forward to lots of buggy fun!

Sincerely,

Colors, Colors Everywhere

Color mixing is one of the earliest science concepts that students learn. There is something almost magical about mixing two colors (like red and yellow) and getting an entirely new color (orange). Colors play an important part in helping students learn to sort objects and make patterns. Activities from this unit also use colors to teach students to follow directions. In a game of Color Clues, children learn word family endings with a color rhyming game. Use *White Rabbit's Color Book* to teach color mixing; try *Color Me a Rhyme: Nature Poems for Young People* to introduce new color words.

Literature Selections

Cleo's Color Book by Stella Blackstone (Barefoot Books, 2010). An orange cat named Cleo spends a day looking at the colors around her. Illustrations are bold and provide great opportunities for exploring color.

Color Me a Rhyme: Nature Poems for Young People by Jane Yolen (Boyds Mills Press, 2003). Yolen's book mixes beautiful photography with a collection of nature poems that use a variety of more complex color words. This is definitely a read-aloud book.

A Color of His Own by Leo Lionni (Knopf Books for Young Readers, 2006). A chameleon suffers an identity crisis because he cannot seem to remain one color, but he finds comfort in the companionship of an older, wiser chameleon.

The Colors of Us by Karen Katz (Henry Holt and Co. BYR Paperbacks, 2007). Celebrate diversity by reading this book, which compares every skin tone in a girl's neighborhood to something wonderful, like peanut butter, chocolate cupcakes, or honey.

White Rabbit's Color Book by Alan Baker (Kingfisher, 1999). What happens when a curious white rabbit finds three cups of paint? Why, she gets a makeover. Rabbit experiments until she creates a new color she finds comfortable.

Pattern Match

Materials: chenille stems, several small containers of wooden beads in a variety of familiar colors

Divide students into pairs. Give each pair two chenille stems and a small container of beads. One student in each pair should string a pattern of beads on a chenille stem, such as yellow-red-blue, yellow-red-blue. The other student should copy the pattern on the other chenille stem. Students should then hold the two chenille stems side-by-side to check that the patterns match. If they do not match, students should work together to correct the second pattern. Once they match, the beads can be removed, and students should reverse roles.

Stop and Go

Materials: tape

Discuss traffic light colors and what they represent. Using tape, mark a starting line on one side of the play area and have students stand on the line. Choose one student to be the police officer. Have her stand with her back to the group on the opposite side of the play area. When the officer says, "Green light," have students move as quickly and quietly as possible toward the police officer until she yells, "Red light!" At this command, students must freeze. As the police officer yells this, she should spin around and try to catch students before they are able to freeze. If she catches anyone who is still moving, that student must return to the starting line and begin again. The first student to reach the officer becomes the next police officer.

Color Mixing

Have students sing or chant the rhyme while following the directions for each color.

Color Mixing

Red makes my feet tap,	(tap feet)
And yellow makes my hands clap.	(clap hands)
But, when I mix red and yellow,	
I get a tappin', clappin' ORANGE!	(tap and clap)
Yellow makes my head shake,	(shake head)
And blue makes my knees quake.	(make knees quiver)
But, when I mix yellow and blue,	
I get a shakin', quakin' GREEN!	(shake and quiver)
Blue makes my hips wiggle,	(wiggle hips)
And red makes my shoulders jiggle.	(jiggle shoulders)
But, when I mix blue and red,	
I get a wigglin', jigglin' PURPLE!	(wiggle and jiggle)

Mixing colors is so much fun,
I could do purple, orange, and green (perform all of the actions together)
Until the day is done!

Color Clues

Materials: index cards, one sheet of paper and set of crayons or markers for each student

Compose a variety of word rhymes about familiar colors. Write each rhyme on an index card. Some sample rhymes include *red bed, blue shoe, yellow fellow, black sack, brown crown, green bean, pink sink, white kite,* and *tan van.* Seat students at tables or on the floor with their drawing paper and crayons. Select a card. Then, give students a clue, such as, "It rhymes with red, and you sleep in it." Players should raise their hands if they think that they know the answer. Call on a student to guess the answer. When the correct answer is given, provide time for students to draw pictures of the answer, using the appropriate color. Repeat with the other game cards.

Variation: For a challenge, have students wait to guess the answer to the riddle until after they have taken time to draw. When everyone is finished drawing, ask for volunteers to hold up their papers and show their answers.

My Three Blocks

Materials: a set of three colorful blocks for each student, small resealable plastic bags

Gather a set of blocks for each student. Each student's set should include three blocks in three different familiar colors, such as red, yellow, and blue. For convenience, place each set in a small bag. Have students sit cross-legged in a circle on the floor. Each student should place his three blocks in front of him. Announce instructions, such as, "Place the red block on top of the yellow block and the blue block on top of the red block," or "Place the yellow block on the left, the blue block in the middle, and the red block on the right." After each set of instructions, give students time to arrange their blocks. You may want to model the correct placement with your own set of blocks, depending on students' developmental levels. After students are all in agreement about the correct arrangement of the blocks, give the next set of instructions. For an extra challenge, let pairs of students race to see who can finish a pattern first.

Graph-a-Pattern

Materials: Graph Paper Pattern (page 75), connecting cubes, crayons

Make a copy of the Graph Paper Pattern for each student. Collect a variety of colorful connecting cubes and crayons in the same colors. Give each student a set of crayons and a copy of the Graph Paper Pattern. Arrange the connecting cubes into a color pattern, such as blue-blue-red-yellow. Each student should duplicate the pattern on the graph paper by coloring one square for each cube. Then, he should complete the rest of the row on the graph paper in the same pattern. When students have finished coloring their patterns, select a student to make a new connecting cube pattern for classmates to duplicate. Continue the game until each student has had a turn to create a new pattern.

Action Colors

Materials: large sheets of construction paper in a variety of familiar colors, tape

Laminate the sheets of construction paper for durability. Give one sheet to each student. (If, for example, there are 16 students in the class and they know eight colors, you can include two sheets of paper for each color and have students perform the activities in pairs.) Tape the sheets of paper randomly on the floor. Make sure that there is plenty of space between the sheets. Assemble students in a circle near the papers. Say a student's name and give her an instruction, such as, "Walk backward to blue," "Hop to red," "Crab walk to yellow," "Gallop to green," or "Skip to orange." After a student performs her action, she should remain standing in that spot while her classmates take their turns. After each student has had a turn and is standing on a sheet of paper, have students return to the circle and start again.

Variation: Play music while students are performing the actions to encourage a variety of movement.

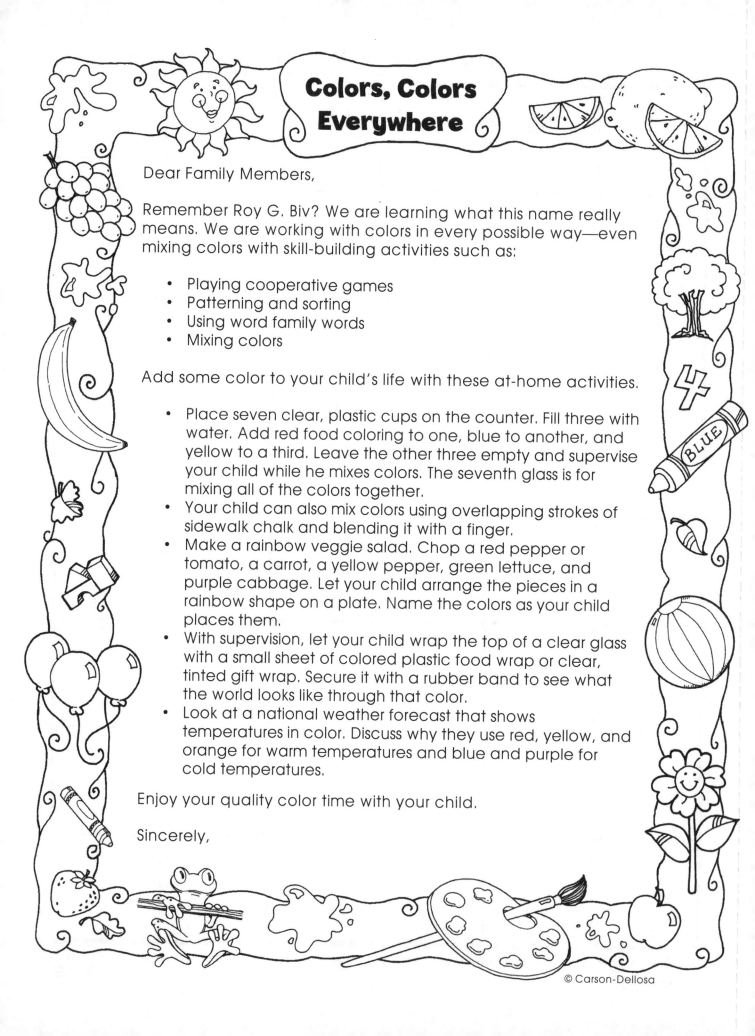

Colors, Colors Everywhere

Dear Family Members,

Remember Roy G. Biv? We are learning what this name really means. We are working with colors in every possible way—even mixing colors with skill-building activities such as:

- Playing cooperative games
- Patterning and sorting
- Using word family words
- Mixing colors

Add some color to your child's life with these at-home activities.

- Place seven clear, plastic cups on the counter. Fill three with water. Add red food coloring to one, blue to another, and yellow to a third. Leave the other three empty and supervise your child while he mixes colors. The seventh glass is for mixing all of the colors together.
- Your child can also mix colors using overlapping strokes of sidewalk chalk and blending it with a finger.
- Make a rainbow veggie salad. Chop a red pepper or tomato, a carrot, a yellow pepper, green lettuce, and purple cabbage. Let your child arrange the pieces in a rainbow shape on a plate. Name the colors as your child places them.
- With supervision, let your child wrap the top of a clear glass with a small sheet of colored plastic food wrap or clear, tinted gift wrap. Secure it with a rubber band to see what the world looks like through that color.
- Look at a national weather forecast that shows temperatures in color. Discuss why they use red, yellow, and orange for warm temperatures and blue and purple for cold temperatures.

Enjoy your quality color time with your child.

Sincerely,

Perhaps because we have never seen them alive, dinosaurs are very captivating for students. The giant size and enormous teeth of some varieties, and the fact that we discover them by digging for bones just like buried treasure, add to the dinosaur's mystique. Use dinosaurs to motivate your students to practice one-to-one correspondence with Dino Dominoes, learn about standard and nonstandard measurement by comparing classroom size to a dinosaur's size, and create interesting dinosaur art. Introduce realistic dinosaurs by reading *My Big Dinosaur Book* and keeping it in a center. Show dinosaurs' sweet, cuddly side with *Danny and the Dinosaur* and *How Do Dinosaurs Say Good Night?*

Literature Selections

Danny and the Dinosaur by Syd Hoff (HarperCollins, 1958). Originally published in 1958, this tale of a boy and his large, prehistoric pal serves as a sweet introduction to dinosaurs.

Dinosaur Roar! by Paul Stickland and Henrietta Stickland (Puffin, 2002). Celebrate dinosaur opposites in a preschool-appropriate book.

How Big Were the Dinosaurs? by Bernard Most (Sandpiper, 1995). Compare the sizes of dinosaurs to familiar objects in this bright and playful book.

How Do Dinosaurs Love Their Cats? by Jane Yolen (Blue Sky Press, 2010). Children will love the silliness of "bad" pet owner behavior as they learn what is involved in keeping a cat happy.

How Do Dinosaurs Say Good Night? by Jane Yolen (Blue Sky Press, 2000). Little dinosaurs try the same tricks as toddlers do when it comes to postponing bedtime. Be sure to look for other books in this series about dinosaurs.

My Big Dinosaur Book by Roger Priddy (St. Martin's Press, 2004). Show students the clear and colorful pictures in this sturdy picture book.

Dinosaurs: What Did They Look Like?

Materials: Dinosaur Pattern (page 82); card stock; crayons or markers; collage materials, such as sequins, glitter, yarn scraps, dried beans, buttons, feathers, and uncooked pasta; glue

Copy the Dinosaur Pattern on card stock for each student. Place the supplies on a table. Explain to students that since dinosaurs are extinct, no one really knows what color they were or what they looked like. Encourage students to color their dinosaurs and add details to make scenery, such as trees, grass, other dinosaurs, and the sky. Then, let them use the collage materials to embellish the dinosaurs. When each student has completed her project, have her name her dinosaur. Help her write the dinosaur's name at the top of her artwork.

Dino Dominoes

Materials: index cards, black marker, dinosaur stickers or stamps

Create 24 index card dominoes by drawing a line down the middle of each card with a black marker. Randomly select eight sections and place one small dinosaur sticker or stamp in each section. Repeat this process using two, three, four, five, and six stickers or stamps. Laminate the cards for durability. Place the dino dominoes on a table. Tell students to shuffle the dominoes and place them facedown on the table. The first player should select a domino and turn it faceup. Player two should select a second domino. If it has a side with the same number of stickers or stamps as

the first domino, players should align the dominoes so that the matching sections touch. Players continue drawing and matching until all of the dominoes are used.

Dino Rub

Materials: Dinosaur Patterns (pages 80–81); crayons; assortment of items with textured surfaces, such as sandpaper, a door mat, corrugated cardboard, linoleum, tile, and a concrete stepping stone

Copy the Dinosaur Patterns for each student. Place the supplies on a table in an art center. Have students place a Dinosaur Pattern over one of the textured surfaces. Ask the student to rub a crayon over the paper to create a textured "skin" for the dinosaur. Encourage students to try different textures for different parts of the dinosaurs and to use the textures when creating a background.

Do the Dino Stomp

Materials: Dinosaur Footprint Pattern (page 83), colorful paper, scissors, crayons or markers, clear packing tape, large sheets of paper

Create a number line to help students practice their math skills. Make 11 copies of the Dinosaur Footprint Pattern on colorful paper. Cut out the patterns and number them from 0 to 10. Laminate the footprints for durability. Place the footprints in order on the floor and tape them with clear packing tape. On large sheets of paper, write basic addition and subtraction problems. Hold up one problem at a time and let students take turns stomping along the footprints to find the answers.

How Big Were the Dinosaurs?

Materials: *How Big Were the Dinosaurs?* by Bernard Most (Sandpiper, 1995), yarn, tape measure

Read *How Big Were the Dinosaurs?* by Bernard Most. This book compares the sizes of different dinosaurs to familiar objects. Some dinosaurs were huge, but some were very small. Have the class vote on a dinosaur to measure. Research how long the dinosaur might have been from head to tail and cut a piece of yarn that long. Then, have students stretch the yarn to its full length. As students are standing at different points along the yarn, tell them where on the dinosaur each might be standing. For example, say, "Tanya is standing at the dinosaur's shoulder."

Move Like a Dinosaur

Materials: lively music

After looking at pictures and discussing different kinds of dinosaurs, it is time to act like dinosaurs. Play music and allow students to move like dinosaurs. Encourage each student to pick a certain kind of dinosaur to mimic. Explain that a tyrannosaurus might move differently from a flying dinosaur or an apatosaurus.

Dinosaur Patterns

Materials: Dinosaur Pattern (page 82), colorful construction paper

Copy the Dinosaur Pattern on three different pieces of colorful paper. Make at least three sets of each color. Since no people lived when dinosaurs existed, we have no idea what color they might have been. Have four to six students hold the colored dinosaurs in a pattern for the rest of the group to see. "Read" the pattern and ask someone to tell what color dinosaur comes next. Ask other students to stand up and hold colorful dinosaurs to continue the pattern.

Ten Hungry Dinosaurs

Materials: Dinosaur Patterns (pages 80–81)

Count on your fingers as you sing this song to the tune of "Ten Little Indians." Use the Dinosaur Patterns to create a finger puppet for each number.

Ten Hungry Dinosaurs

One hungry, two hungry, three hungry dinosaurs,
Four hungry, five hungry, six hungry dinosaurs,
Seven hungry, eight hungry, nine hungry dinosaurs,
Ten hungry dinosaurs.

Dinosaur Patterns

Dinosaur Patterns

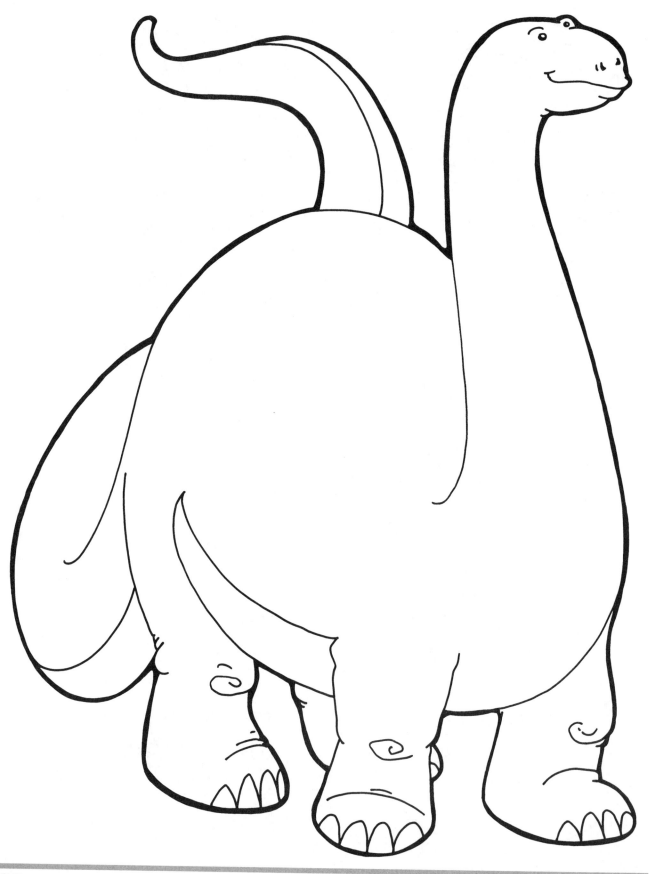

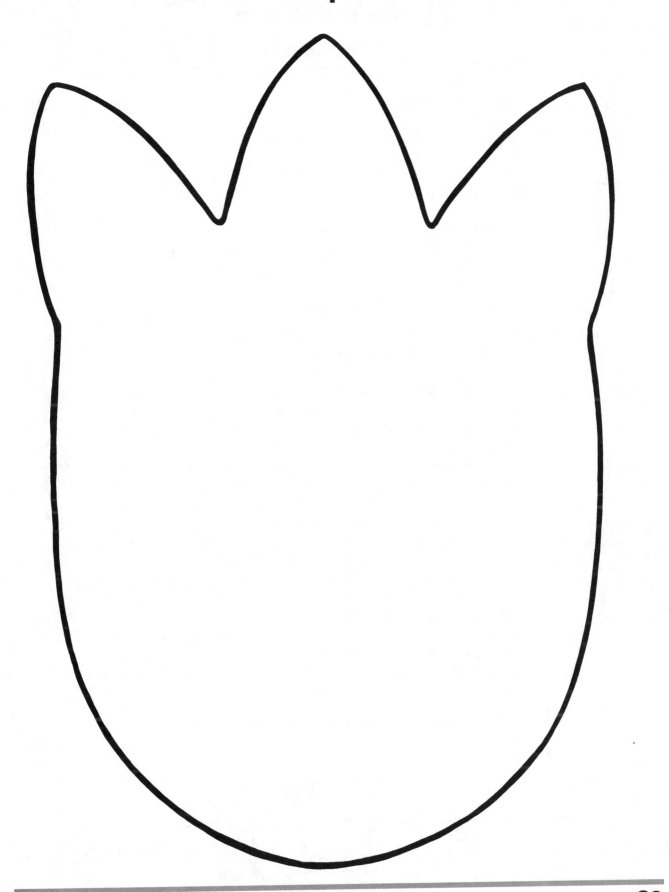

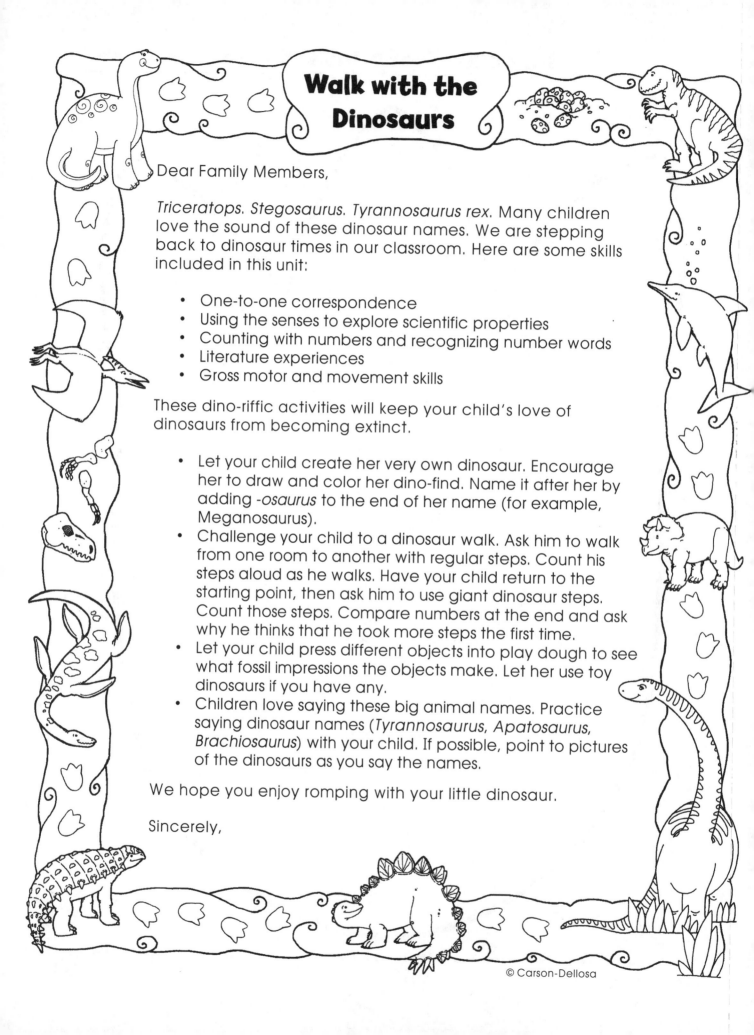

Walk with the Dinosaurs

Dear Family Members,

Triceratops. Stegosaurus. Tyrannosaurus rex. Many children love the sound of these dinosaur names. We are stepping back to dinosaur times in our classroom. Here are some skills included in this unit:

- One-to-one correspondence
- Using the senses to explore scientific properties
- Counting with numbers and recognizing number words
- Literature experiences
- Gross motor and movement skills

These dino-riffic activities will keep your child's love of dinosaurs from becoming extinct.

- Let your child create her very own dinosaur. Encourage her to draw and color her dino-find. Name it after her by adding *-osaurus* to the end of her name (for example, Meganosaurus).
- Challenge your child to a dinosaur walk. Ask him to walk from one room to another with regular steps. Count his steps aloud as he walks. Have your child return to the starting point, then ask him to use giant dinosaur steps. Count those steps. Compare numbers at the end and ask why he thinks that he took more steps the first time.
- Let your child press different objects into play dough to see what fossil impressions the objects make. Let her use toy dinosaurs if you have any.
- Children love saying these big animal names. Practice saying dinosaur names (*Tyrannosaurus, Apatosaurus, Brachiosaurus*) with your child. If possible, point to pictures of the dinosaurs as you say the names.

We hope you enjoy romping with your little dinosaur.

Sincerely,

Down on the Farm

Students and adults alike are drawn to farms. They represent a simpler way of life to many people. It is also fascinating to know where most of our food originates from, and to see the domestic animals so often found in favorite children's books. The lure of farm animals can motivate students to practice animal recognition and animal sounds, farm role-playing, using descriptive language, critical thinking skills, geometry, and scientific exploration. Show real farm animal photographs from the book *Farm Animals*, and tell some funny farm tales with the other selections. Use *Inside a Barn in the Country* for sequencing practice.

Literature Selections

Click, Clack, Moo: Cows That Type by Doreen Cronin (Simon & Schuster Children's Publishing, 2000). The cows are cold, and they are demanding electric blankets. Farmer Brown does not want to compromise, but Duck acts as the mediator and moves negotiations along.

The Day Jimmy's Boa Ate the Wash by Trinka Hakes Noble (Puffin, 1992). Jimmy's class takes a field trip to a farm, but in this story told in reverse, it is his pet boa constrictor that steals the show.

Farm Animals (DK Publishing, 2004). Excellent photography documents a group of children visiting a farm.

Inside a Barn in the Country by Alyssa Satin Capucilli (Scholastic, 1995). Parents and children who are familiar with the cumulative tale "This Is the House That Jack Built" will recognize a similar storytelling device here. When a cat chases a mouse, all of the other sleeping animals are dragged into the mix.

Mrs. Wishy-Washy's Farm by Joy Cowley (Puffin, 2006). Mrs. Wishy-Washy loves to wash everything, including her farm creatures. When the farm animals run off to the big city, they find lots of trouble! All is soon well as they are rescued and returned home.

Walk This Way

Materials: Farm Animal Cards (page 88), card stock, crayons or markers, scissors, cowbell

Copy the Farm Animal Cards onto sturdy card stock. Color the cards with crayons or markers and cut them apart. Laminate the cards for durability. Place the cards and the cowbell on a table. Let one student be in charge of the cards and cowbell. Have the other students pretend to be farm animals. Tell the student with the cards to select one card from the stack, show the class, and say the name of the pictured animal. The other students should begin to act, move, and make sounds like the animal. When the student selects a new card, he should ring the cowbell to notify the others of the change.

Down on the Farm

Materials: variety of blocks, small farm animal figurines, toy farm vehicles

Place the supplies in a center. Encourage students to create a farm scene using the blocks. Suggest building a barn, fences, and feed troughs. Tell students that they can also use the toy farm animals and farming equipment vehicles as part of the scene.

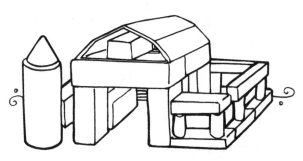

Who Said That?

Materials: Farm Animal Cards (page 88), card stock, crayons or markers, scissors, premade CD of animal sounds, CD player, headphones

Obtain or make a CD of the sounds made by each animal featured on the Farm Animal Cards. There should be a long pause between each sound. Copy the Farm Animal Cards onto card stock. Color the cards with crayons or markers and cut them apart. Laminate the cards for durability. Place the cards and other supplies in a center. To play, a student should spread the nine cards faceup in front of her. Then, she should listen to the first animal sound on the CD using the headphones. When she recognizes the sound, she should turn that animal's card facedown and wait for the next sound. Play continues until all nine cards are facedown.

Variation: Instead of using the CD, have a second player join the game. You will need two sets of Farm Animal Cards. One student should spread her cards in front of her as directed above. The second player should hold the other stack in his lap. Player two should look at the top card and then make the sound of that animal for player one. Player one must then turn the corresponding card facedown. Play continues until player one has turned all of her cards facedown. Have players switch roles and play again.

Mixed-up Barnyard

Materials: Farm Animal Cards (page 88), scissors

Make enough copies of the Farm Animal Cards for each student to have one card. Tell students that the only sounds that they can make are the sounds of the animals on their cards. Explain that the object of the activity is to wander around and find all of the matching animals by listening for the correct sound. Remind students that they cannot make any sounds other than their animal sounds. Once a student finds another student with the matching animal card, encourage them to hold hands and stick together until they find the other matching animals.

Farms Feed Us

Materials: Barn Pattern (page 89), Farm Patterns (page 90), crayons or markers, scissors

Ask students to name the animals and things that are found on a farm. Copy and color the Barn Pattern and place it where students can see it. Ask students what things they might find in a barn. They may name animals and farm equipment. Tell them that there are different kinds of farms. Farms provide grocery stores with the food that we buy, like milk, vegetables, fruit, meat, and grains. Show each picture and place it by the barn as you talk about the different farm products shown on copies of the Farm Patterns.

Animals Around the Farm

Sing to the tune of "The Wheels on the Bus." Have students move around and act like the animal as they sing.

Animals Around the Farm

The cow in the barn goes *moo, moo, moo,*
Moo, moo, moo, moo, moo, moo.
The cow in the barn goes *moo, moo, moo,*
All around the farm.

Additional verses:
The duck in the pond goes *quack, quack, quack.* . . . all around the farm.
The pig in the mud goes *oink, oink, oink.* . . . all around the farm.
The hen in the coop goes *cluck, cluck, cluck.* . . . all around the farm.
The sheep in the hay goes *baa, baa, baa.* . . . all around the farm.

Farm Boogie Woogie

Materials: Farm Animal Cards (page 88), scissors

Make two copies of the Farm Animal Cards. Give one to each student. If you have an odd number of students, give three copies of one animal. Students should secretly observe the animal pictures on their cards and hide them. When you say "Farm boogie woogie," students should pretend to be the animals on their cards. They may make the sound as well as act like the animal. Without using any words, they must find the person who is acting like the same animal. The matching pair of students should then separate from the rest of the group and watch while the others find their matching partner.

cow

horse

goose

chicken

sheep

goat

dog

cat

pig

Down on the Farm

Dear Family Members,

For many children, farms are wonderful. It is where much of their food comes from and where many of their favorite animals live. In our classroom, we are learning how farms work and how they help us. We are also engaging in these topics:

- Imaginative and cooperative play
- Activities that teach about health and nutrition
- Community awareness activities
- Basic geometry practice
- Animal sound recognition

Sow the seeds of creativity with these at-home farm activities.

- Plant a seed or two of your own. Ask your child to help save some seeds from a few fresh vegetables. Fill a disposable cup with potting soil. Let your child cover the seeds. Place the cup in a sunny, warm spot and water gently every few days.
- Children will love to muck out the barn! Give your child a toy rake, clean dustpan, large feed scoop, or plastic shovel. Push a few chairs close together to create space for a stall. Then, pile throw pillows, soft blocks, cardboard boxes, or crumpled newspaper on the floor between the chairs. Tell your child that the horse's hay needs to be cleaned out. Give him the shovel and tell him to muck out the barn (shovel the "dirty hay"). When he is finished, he can shovel the objects back in the barn as "clean hay."
- If you have plastic food, play a harvest game. Have your child leave the room. Scatter the food around the room, and then have your child return. Give her a basket and time her to see how long it takes her to "harvest" the food. When she is finished, let her "plant" the food for you to harvest.

Enjoy the freshly picked fun with your little farmer.

Sincerely,

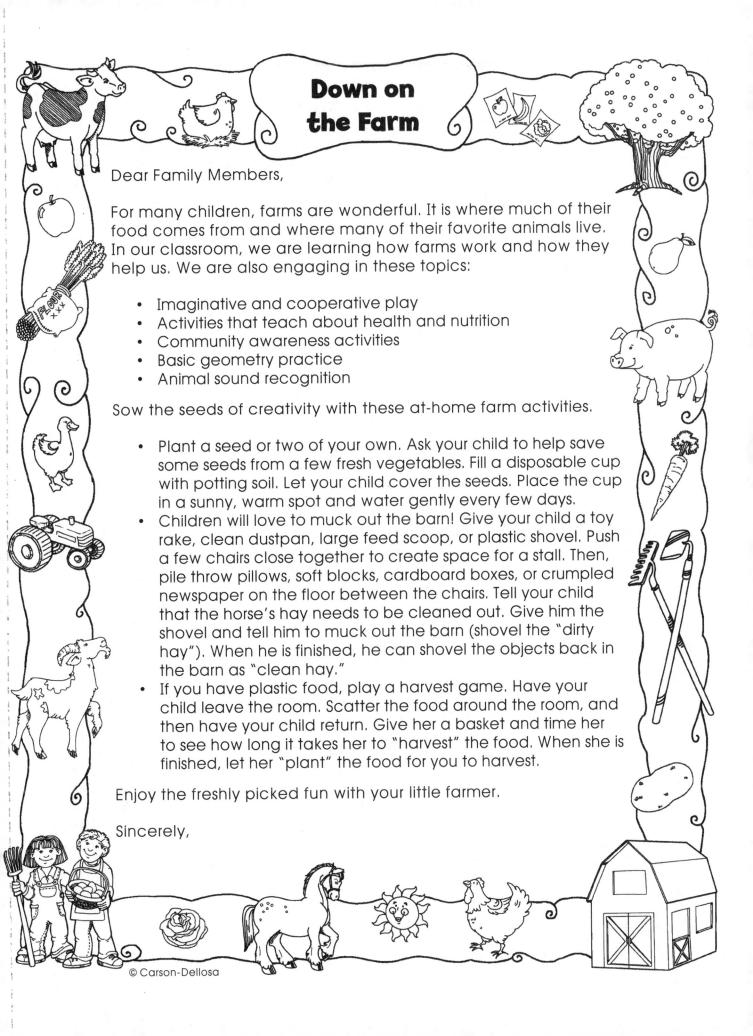

There is a reason that taking a nature walk is on preschool teachers' lists of favorite activities. Students love being outside, and there is no better place for them to satisfy their curiosity about everything that they see. While working with nature, you can inspire students to role-play about gardens, use scientific observation to learn more about worms and dirt, and discover and discuss new knowledge about trees and water. Introduce students to the water cycle with *The Snowflake: A Water Cycle Story*, and share the joy of growing flowers and gardens with the other reading selections. Consider planting a class garden as you read from these books.

Literature Selections

From Seed to Plant by Gail Gibbons (Holiday House, 1993). Early readers get a simple, clear introduction to pollination and other aspects of plant reproduction.

Jack's Garden by Henry Cole (Greenwillow Books, 1997). Jack plants and harvests a backyard garden in this cumulative tale.

Planting a Rainbow by Lois Ehlert (Sandpiper, 1992). A beautifully illustrated book that celebrates the cyclical nature of a flower garden.

A Seed Grows: My First Look at a Plant's Life Cycle by Pamela Hickman (Kids Can Press, 1997). Seeds start small and grow into amazing and useful plants. This book has interactive flaps and contains pictures of each plant's underground growth.

The Snowflake: A Water Cycle Story by Neil Waldman (Millbrook Press, 2003). Students will understand the water cycle as they listen to you read about a snowflake making its journey from nature to a bathroom sink and back to nature again, with many stops in between.

Flower Necklaces

Materials: construction paper or foam cut into flower shapes (available at craft stores), hole punch, 3 bowls, yarn, 1 wooden bead per student, masking tape, plastic drinking straws, fruit-flavored cereal rings

Punch a hole in the center of each flower shape and put it in a bowl. Cut an 18" (46 cm) piece of yarn for each student. Tie a wooden bead onto one end of each piece of yarn. Wrap a piece of masking tape around the other end for easy threading. Cut plastic drinking straws into 1" (2.5 cm) lengths. Place the straws and cereal rings in separate bowls and place the supplies on a table. Allow students to string flowers, cereal rings, and straw pieces onto their yarn as desired. Encourage students to use patterning skills while stringing the flowers, straws, and cereal.

 **(See page 2.)**

Gardening

Materials: large tarp, newsprint, paper shredder, large bucket or trash can, plastic flowerpots, artificial flowers, watering cans, seed packets, dirt, toy food, plastic or toy gardening tools, garden hose, toy wheelbarrow or wagon, small plastic fencing, dustpan and broom, baskets, garden gloves

Place a large tarp on the floor. Shred newsprint in a paper shredder to create "dirt" or "mulch," and put it in a large bucket or trash can. Create a table for potting flowers with empty plastic pots, artificial flowers, watering cans, seed packets, and plenty of "dirt." Create a vegetable garden by placing the toy food in rows on the tarp and covering them with the newsprint dirt. Encourage students to dig the vegetables, pretend to plant more seeds, and water them with the hose while others plant flowers in the flowerpots.

Worms and Dirt

Materials: sensory table filled with dirt, gravel, and sand; rubber fishing worms (without hooks); measuring cups; sifters; slotted spoons

Fill a sensory table with dirt, gravel, and sand. Mix them together, or separate them into sections. Bury several worms in the dirt, gravel, and sand. Place the other supplies on top of the mixture. Allow students to sift through the table using their bare hands, the cups, sifters, and slotted spoons. Encourage students to describe what they see, hear, smell, and feel as they explore in the sensory table.

Flower "Magic"

Materials: white carnation, vase, water, food coloring

Cut the bottom of a white carnation stem. Place the stem in a clear vase of water. Add a few drops of food coloring. Ask students to predict what will happen. Leave the vase in a secure place where students can observe it throughout the rest of the day and the next day. Describe any changes that you observe. Explain that the flower stem contains veins that carry water from the roots to the flower. Students can see this happen when the colored water moves up the stem and into the petals.

Fresh Flowers

Materials: fragrant flower petals, fresh flowers, magnifying glasses, poster or book of flowers

Distribute soft and fragrant flower petals, such as rose petals, to students. Let students experience the feel and smell of the flowers. Then, discuss the colors and shapes of the petals. Talk about flowers. What color flowers have they seen? What kinds of flowers can they name and describe? It is helpful to have a poster of different flowers or a book with color photos of different flowers. Look at different shades of the same color. Do flowers come in all colors of the spectrum? Bring in samples of flowers that are currently in bloom. Compare the sizes, shapes, colors, and smells of different flowers. Have students look for flower details with a magnifying glass. Point to the veins in the petals, the reproductive parts, and the inside of the stem (if cut). Allow each student to talk about what she sees and ask questions.

 **(See page 2.)**

Trees Are Important!

Materials: paint, paper, paintbrushes

Discuss the importance of trees. We use trees for shade and beauty as well as food. Animals use trees for homes and food. Trees and other plants also provide us with air to breathe. Have students help you think of things that grow on trees, such as apples, pears, oranges, lemons, walnuts, and bananas. Discuss the reasons that trees are sometimes cut down. Tree roots can do a lot of damage to houses or sidewalks. Branches can get in the way of power lines or create too much shade in a yard. Once a tree is cut down, it also has many uses, such as firewood, lumber for building, and wood for toys, tools, paper, and boxes. Some people cut down forest trees for a specific use. But, when they do that, they must cut only some of the trees and plant new ones to replace what they cut. If all of the trees in a forest are cut down, the forest will be gone along with many animal homes. It takes many years for a tree to grow. Ask students to close their eyes and picture a tree that they know. What do they like about that tree? What does the tree look like, feel like, smell like, sound like? What kind is it and what is it used for? If possible, go outside and look at trees. Let students stretch their arms around a tree, feel its bark, and study what it looks like. Count the number of leaves on a branch or the number of branches on a small tree. Older students can measure the width of trees. Study the tree carefully so that students can go inside and paint pictures of it.

 **(See page 2.)**

Fruits and Vegetables

Materials: pictures of fruit trees and vegetable gardens

Show pictures of fruit trees and vegetable gardens. Ask students to name their favorite vegetables and fruits. Discuss the different ways that they are prepared. Vegetables and fruits can be eaten raw or cooked. Discuss the importance of eating vegetables and fruits every day. Vitamins and minerals keep you healthy. Different fruits and vegetables provide different vitamins and minerals, so it is important to eat a variety of foods. Discuss the different ways that fruits and vegetables grow: on trees, bushes, plants, and underground. Can students recall how their favorite fruits and vegetables grow?

Eat Your Fruits and Veggies!

Have students pretend to eat different fruits and vegetables that you name. Encourage them to act out everything from preparation to reacting to the taste. For example, if you say *watermelon*, they may first carry the heavy melon, cut it into slices, bite the slice, and spit out the seeds. Choose some foods that will get a strong reaction. A lemon may produce some wonderful sour faces, while broccoli will produce both positive and negative reactions. You may wish to have half the class act at a time, while the other half observes, then switch roles as you move to the next food.

Water Is Important!

Materials: maps and photos of bodies of water

Ask students to discuss all of the uses for water, such as for drinking, cooking, bathing, swimming, boating, watering plants, and washing clothes and dishes and as rain and a home for animals. Tell students that most of the water on Earth is salt water that we cannot drink. Much of the water that is fresh is polluted. Explain that water is a very important resource to us, so it is essential that we work to keep it clean. Talk about ways that water gets polluted. Ask students to think of things that they can do to reduce water pollution.

Extension: Ask students, "How many different bodies of water can you name?" Talk about ways that we find water in nature: ponds, streams, creeks, rivers, lakes, puddles, oceans, waterfalls, swamps, and so on. Listen to students' water experiences. Also, discuss proper names of these places, such as the Atlantic Ocean, Lake Michigan, the Mississippi River, and so on. It is helpful to have maps and photos to help students understand the relative sizes of these different bodies of water.

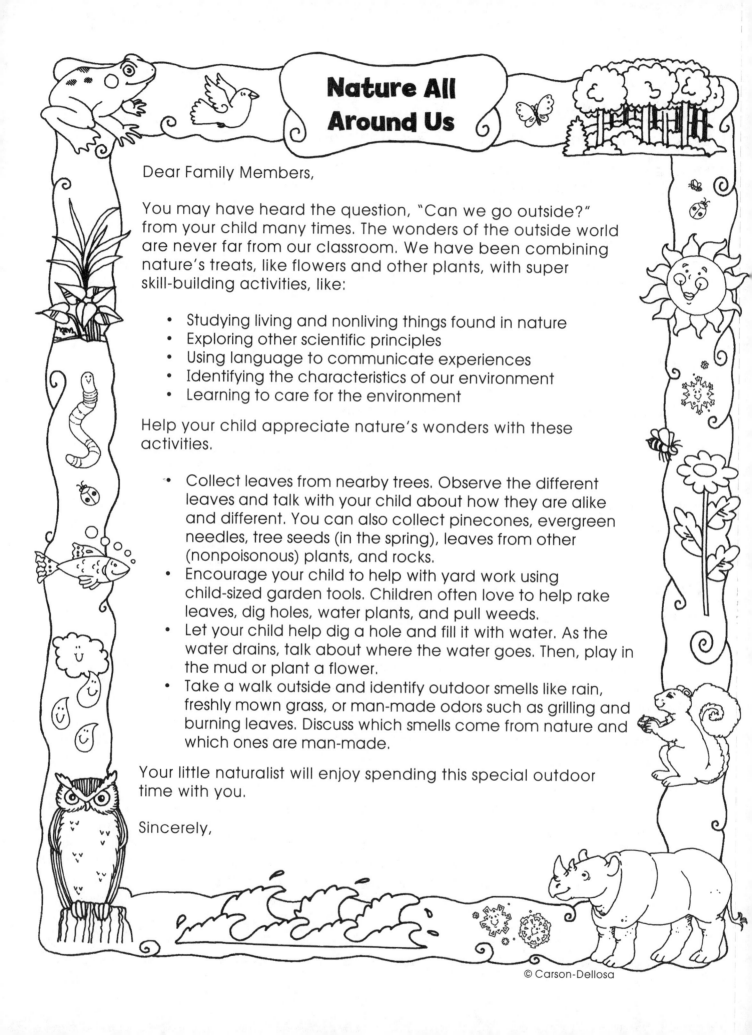

Nature All Around Us

Dear Family Members,

You may have heard the question, "Can we go outside?" from your child many times. The wonders of the outside world are never far from our classroom. We have been combining nature's treats, like flowers and other plants, with super skill-building activities, like:

- Studying living and nonliving things found in nature
- Exploring other scientific principles
- Using language to communicate experiences
- Identifying the characteristics of our environment
- Learning to care for the environment

Help your child appreciate nature's wonders with these activities.

- Collect leaves from nearby trees. Observe the different leaves and talk with your child about how they are alike and different. You can also collect pinecones, evergreen needles, tree seeds (in the spring), leaves from other (nonpoisonous) plants, and rocks.
- Encourage your child to help with yard work using child-sized garden tools. Children often love to help rake leaves, dig holes, water plants, and pull weeds.
- Let your child help dig a hole and fill it with water. As the water drains, talk about where the water goes. Then, play in the mud or plant a flower.
- Take a walk outside and identify outdoor smells like rain, freshly mown grass, or man-made odors such as grilling and burning leaves. Discuss which smells come from nature and which ones are man-made.

Your little naturalist will enjoy spending this special outdoor time with you.

Sincerely,

Autumn Awaits

After the long, warm days of summer, the brisk nights and crisp days of autumn seem to almost crackle with excitement. Popular themes include harvest, pumpkins, autumn leaves, and yes, back-to-school when everything is new again. This theme easily lends itself to skill-building activities like doing science experiments with blowing wind, role-playing some autumn fun, singing autumn-themed songs and rhymes, matching and graphing with apples and leaves, and even working on fine motor skills with spicy and fragrant play dough. Highlight autumn preparations by animals and humans in books like *Animals in the Fall* and *It's Fall*. If you plan any pumpkin activities, such as carving, counting seeds, or role-playing, include *It's Pumpkin Time!* as the book of the day.

Literature Selections

Animals in the Fall by Gail Saunders-Smith (Capstone Press, 2000). Crisp photographs show the winter preparations made during autumn by animals, people, and plants.

It's Fall by Linda Glaser (Millbrook Press, 2001). A boy explores all of the changes that come with autumn, including wearing warmer clothes, watching the trees lose their leaves, and noticing the days getting shorter and shorter.

It's Pumpkin Time! by Zoe Hall (Scholastic Paperbacks, 1999). Follow a pumpkin's journey from seedling to jack-o'-lantern.

Leaf Man by Lois Ehlert (Harcourt Children's Books, 2005). Ehlert uses amazing leaf collages to tell the story of a group of leaves as they blow over the landscape.

Little Red's Autumn Adventure by Sarah The Duchess of York Ferguson (Simon & Schuster Children's Publishing, 2009). Little Red and her friends find great adventure on their way to the Great Harvest Festival in Bluebell Wood. From kicking up the golden leaves to leaf-boarding down the hill, there is fun for everyone.

It Feels Like Autumn!

Materials: assortment of autumn items, such as leaves, acorns, pinecones, sticks, small gourds or pumpkins, and pumpkin seeds; sensory table

Place the autumn items in the sensory table. Encourage students to sort, examine, and manipulate the autumn items. Ask them to describe similarities and differences among the items. Remind students to be careful because items like pinecones and sticks may have prickly edges or sharp ends.

 **(See page 2.)**

Autumn Dough

Materials: salt dough or play dough; resealable plastic bags; yellow, red, orange, and brown powdered tempera paint; saltshakers; plastic place mats; spices, such as ground cinnamon, cloves, allspice, and nutmeg; autumn-themed cookie cutters, such as leaves, pumpkins, and apples

Place a handful of dough in each plastic bag. Pour a small amount of powdered tempera paint into each saltshaker. Place all of the supplies on a table. Each student should remove the dough from one bag and place it on a plastic place mat. Then, she should choose a saltshaker and sprinkle a small amount of powdered paint onto the dough. Have her roll and knead the dough to mix in the paint until the desired color is achieved. Then, have her select a spice and sprinkle a small amount onto the dough. She should roll and knead it into the dough as well. When the dough balls are colored and scented, students can make shapes with the cookie cutters, mix small amounts of the different doughs together to achieve new scents and colors, and mold a variety of their own shapes.

 (See page 2.)

Positive and Negative Leaf Prints

Materials: tempera paint, aluminum pie pans, variety of autumn leaves (real or artificial), newspaper, sponge paintbrushes, white construction paper

Pour the paint into aluminum pie pans. Place all of the supplies on a table. Have each student place a leaf on a piece of newspaper. Instruct him to brush paint onto the leaf until it is completely covered. Then, help him carefully lift the leaf, flip it over, and make a print on a sheet of construction paper. Encourage students to experiment with overlapping leaves, different shapes and sizes of leaves, various brushstrokes and patterns. Set aside the papers to dry.

Variation: Have each student place a small, rolled-up piece of masking tape on one side to temporarily attach a leaf to his paper. Then, tell him to brush paint from the middle of the leaf onto the white construction paper. He should brush all of  the way around the leaf in this manner. Then, instruct him to remove the leaf and discard it. A leaf outline surrounded by brushed paint will remain on his paper.

 (See page 2.)

Autumn Shakers

Materials: bowls; assorted autumn nature items, such as hay, acorns, leaves, and twigs; paper lunch bags; twist ties or rubber bands; crayons or markers

Place each type of nature item into a separate bowl. Place the supplies on a table. Give each student two paper bags to decorate. Next, have him choose two different items from nature and place each into a separate bag. Help him close the bags with the twist ties. Be sure to leave some air in the bags. Then, tell each student to shake his bag to hear the differences in the sounds.

Extension: Prepare two paper bags of each type of item. Close the bags and place them on a table. Encourage students to try to match the bags by listening to the sounds they make when they are shaken.

Leaf Exploration

Materials: basket or box of various autumn leaves, magnifying glass, pencils and crayons, paper

Place the leaves in the basket. Place all of the supplies on a table. Tell students to select several different leaves from the basket and examine them with and without the magnifying glass. Encourage students to compare the sizes, shapes, and colors; feel the veins and edges; and smell, manipulate, and crumble the leaves. Have students draw or trace their favorite leaves on sheets of paper. Ask students if the smell of the leaves reminds them of anything. Let each student write or dictate their answers next to their tracings.

 **(See page 2.)**

Pumpkin Patch

Materials: medium-sized cardboard boxes, yellow bulletin board paper; tape; boxes; assortment of real or artificial pumpkins and other gourds; money manipulatives; wagon; digital scale; farm costumes, such as overalls, straw hats, bandanas, or work gloves

Wrap medium-sized cardboard boxes, such as empty copy paper boxes, in yellow bulletin board paper to represent hay bales. Stack the "hay bales," scatter the pumpkins and gourds to represent a pumpkin patch, and display the scale and wagon for shoppers and workers. Encourage students to choose roles as farmers and shoppers. Farmers can help customers select pumpkins, weigh the pumpkins, determine the prices, and give hay rides in the wagon. They can also create hay bale mazes for customers to navigate.

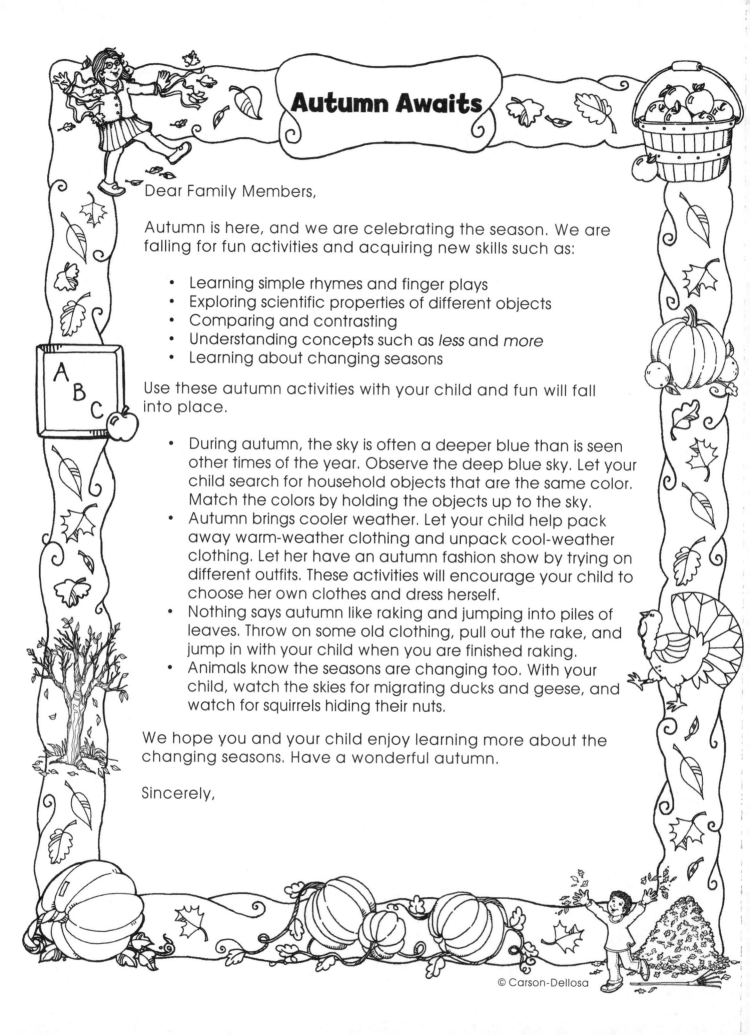

Autumn Awaits

Dear Family Members,

Autumn is here, and we are celebrating the season. We are falling for fun activities and acquiring new skills such as:

- Learning simple rhymes and finger plays
- Exploring scientific properties of different objects
- Comparing and contrasting
- Understanding concepts such as *less* and *more*
- Learning about changing seasons

Use these autumn activities with your child and fun will fall into place.

- During autumn, the sky is often a deeper blue than is seen other times of the year. Observe the deep blue sky. Let your child search for household objects that are the same color. Match the colors by holding the objects up to the sky.
- Autumn brings cooler weather. Let your child help pack away warm-weather clothing and unpack cool-weather clothing. Let her have an autumn fashion show by trying on different outfits. These activities will encourage your child to choose her own clothes and dress herself.
- Nothing says autumn like raking and jumping into piles of leaves. Throw on some old clothing, pull out the rake, and jump in with your child when you are finished raking.
- Animals know the seasons are changing too. With your child, watch the skies for migrating ducks and geese, and watch for squirrels hiding their nuts.

We hope you and your child enjoy learning more about the changing seasons. Have a wonderful autumn.

Sincerely,

Winter Wonders

If you live in an area where it gets cold and snowy, there is great anticipation in waiting for that first snowfall. Winter holidays and the long break from school make the season even more enjoyable. Keep restless students engaged with fun, winter-themed activities such as creating "snow" art, studying how water freezes, snowball play, mitten matching, and winter rhymes and finger plays. If you get to venture in the snow with students, have them try some of the activities featured in the literature, such as following footprints, shaking snow from trees, and building a snowman. Pair a reading of *The Mitten* with the mitten pattern activities. And of course, when you read a story, consider providing small cups of warm cocoa and cookies to really set the mood.

Literature Selections

A Penguin Story by Antoinette Portis (HarperCollins, 2008). Edna the Penguin sets off on a quest to find adventure and discovers a camp of Antarctic scientists. Pages are beautifully designed with bold geometric designs of the Antarctic landscapes.

The First Day of Winter by Denise Fleming (Henry Holt and Co., 2005). A snowman narrates the story of gifts brought to him by the little boys who built him. This is a warm, friendly book for the coldest season.

The Mitten by Jan Brett (Scholastic, 1990). Nicki loses his brand-new white mitten in the snow, just as his grandmother feared. When Nicki finds it again, it is stretched to several times its size, having become a home to a group of chilly wild animals. Brett's ornate art is a favorite with students.

Snow by Uri Shulevitz (Farrar, Straus and Giroux, 2004). Although the forecasters and other doubters are certain no snow will fall, a little boy and his dog find otherwise as they rush outside in anticipation of the first few flakes of a really impressive snowfall.

The Snowy Day by Ezra Jack Keats (Puffin, 1976). In this Caldecott Medal winner, a small boy awakens to find his city covered with snow. Keats's young hero experiments with saving a snowball, making a snow angel, and knocking snow from a tree. Any student who loves snow will be familiar with all of these fun activities.

Tracks in the Snow by Wong Herbert Yee (Square Fish, 2007). Who made those tracks in the snow? A little girl ventures out with her animal companions to solve this gentle winter mystery. All ends well with tea and cookies.

Snowball Toss

Materials: several white, mismatched socks; large box

Gather a variety of white, mismatched socks. Roll them into balls or tie them in knots. Have students form a line next to the pile of "snowballs." Place a large box a short distance away. One at a time, see how many snowballs each student can toss in the box without missing. Each time a student tosses a snowball into the box, have her take a step backward before tossing the next snowball. See how far away she can stand and still accurately toss a snowball. Or, let students try tossing the socks backward over their heads into the box, through their legs, or with their eyes closed.

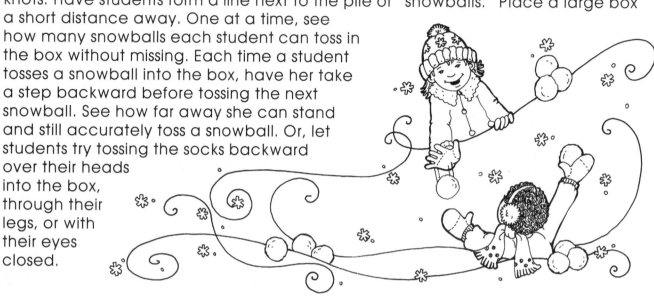

How Many Snowballs?

Materials: Snowman Pattern (page 103), glue, cotton balls, pencils

How many snowballs does it take to make a snowman? Give each student a copy of the Snowman Pattern, glue, and cotton balls. Have students guess how many cotton balls they will need to cover their snowman. Help each student write the number on his snowman's hat. Then, let students glue cotton balls to the snowmen. When they are finished, have students count how many cotton balls they used and compare the totals to their estimates. (If desired, have students count the cotton balls as they work instead of counting when they are finished.) Depending on students' counting skills, you may want to make reduced copies of the Snowman Pattern so that each student will not need as many cotton balls to complete the activity. Or, have students count how many cotton balls it takes to complete the perimeters of the snowmen.

Winter Wonders

Dear Family Members,

It is cold outside! We are having a blast learning about the coldest season. We are warming up during our "Winter Wonders" unit with some cozy, fun activities that keep us moving, like:

- Learning about changing seasons
- Estimating and predicting
- Fine motor skill acquisition
- Creating two- and three-dimensional art
- Counting, matching, and patterning

Enjoy chilly days by joining your child in some wintery fun.

- Talk with your child about what makes him warmer: blankets, warm drinks, hugs, a fire in the fireplace. Let your child choose his favorite warm-up method, then do it together. Snuggle under blankets, make mugs of hot chocolate, or think of a new method.
- Fresh air and exercise during the short, dark days of winter will help keep your child healthy and happy. Encourage your child to dress warmly and play outside during the winter.
- Be sure to remember your animal friends during the cold weather. Fill bird and squirrel feeders. Birds are very easy to spot against the frosty or snowy ground.
- Give a science lesson while skid-proofing your stairs. Explain that salt water (like ocean water) has a lower freezing point than regular water. Let your child help you sprinkle rock salt on icy steps, then watch the ice melt.

If your child gets tired of the cold weather, remind your child that spring is just around the corner.

Sincerely,

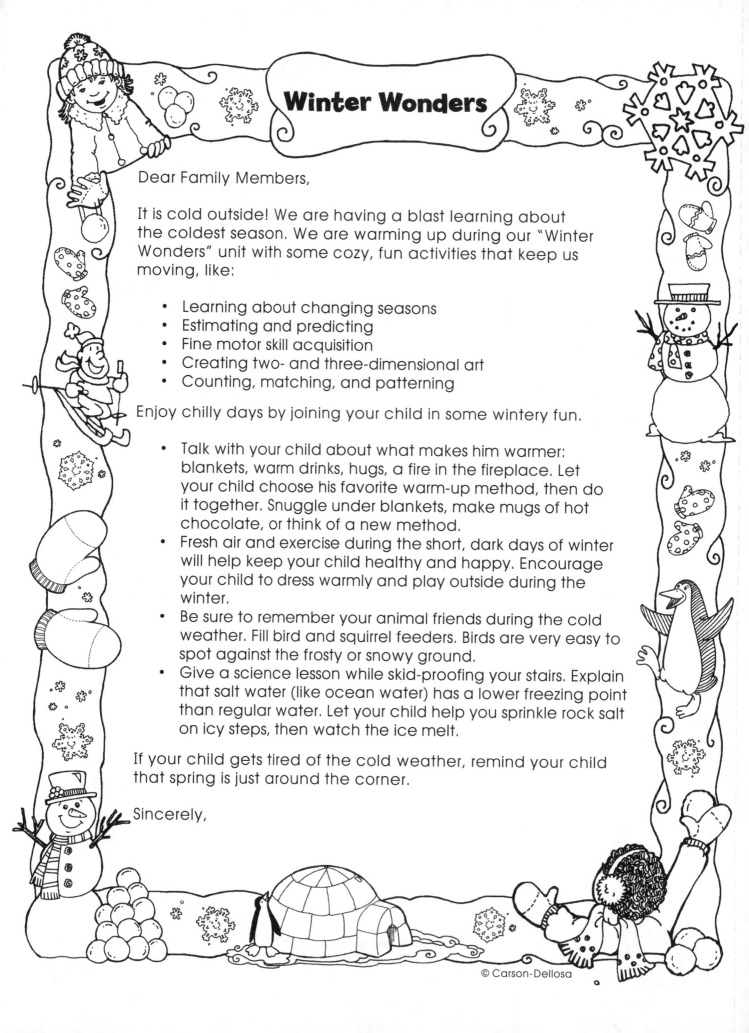

After a long, cold winter, spring truly feels like a breath of fresh air. As the days grow longer and the weather gets warmer, students will be looking forward to activities that deal with the changing seasons, the appearance of baby animals, and springtime activities and holidays. Celebrate spring in your classroom while also helping students learn counting skills, examine properties of water, and even dance around the Maypole. After reading *My Spring Robin*, take students outside to see if they can spot a robin. If your school or child care designates a rest period, try starting it by reading *When will it be spring?* to calm any restless students. Have them pretend to successfully hibernate after the story is finished.

Literature Selections

It's Spring! by Linda Glaser (Millbrook Press, 2002). Illustrated with cut paper and painting, this book catalogs the best things about spring for students.

My Spring Robin by Anne Rockwell (Aladdin, 1996). While searching for a robin, a little girl encounters many other signs of spring in her backyard.

Red Sings from Treetops: A Year in Colors by Joyce Sidman (Houghton Mifflin Books for Children, 2009). Throughout this book about seasons, mixed media illustrations provide much to look at. All of the senses are included as colors evoke vivid smells and textures. This book has a powerful visual impact.

Spring Is Here by Taro Gomi (Chronicle Books, 2006). A white cat that literally changes with the seasons is the star of this simply worded picture book.

When will it be spring? by Catherine Walters (Little Tiger Press, 1998). Just like a preschooler, Alfie the bear cub just cannot seem to settle down and hibernate. The prospect of spring is just too exciting! His mother patiently explains that the signs of spring that he thinks he sees outside the den are really snowflakes and a campfire glow.

Counting Flowers

Materials: index cards, marker, assorted artificial flowers (available at craft stores), large box or basket, 10 plastic vases

Use index cards to label the vases from 1 to 10. Place the flowers in the box or basket. Place the flowers and vases on a table. Have students count aloud as they put the appropriate number of flowers in each vase. Then, have students remove the flowers, rearrange the vases, and start over.

Extension: Label the vases with simple math facts, such as *1 + 1*. Have students solve the math facts and place the correct number of flowers in the vases.

Fabulous Flower Matching

Materials: Flower, Stem, and Flowerpot Patterns (page 107), colorful paper, scissors, glue, marker

Make 11 copies of the Flower, Stem, and Flowerpot Patterns on colorful paper. Cut out the pieces and glue the flowers to the stems. Label each flower with a number from 0 to 10 and label each flowerpot with a number set from 0 to 10. Laminate the pieces for durability. Give each student a flower or a flowerpot. Have students stand or sit in a large circle. Choose a student with a flowerpot pattern and have him place it on the floor in the middle of the circle. Ask the student with the matching flower to plant it in the flowerpot. Continue until all of the flowers have been "planted". Then, redistribute the pieces. Students who had flowers in the first round should have flowerpots in the second round so that all students have a chance to "plant" flowers.

Potting Plants

Materials: scissors; floral foam; sturdy, plastic flowerpots; marker; pairs of child-sized gardening gloves; gardening hats; aprons (optional); artificial flowers (available at craft stores)

Cut a floral foam circle to fit securely inside each flowerpot. Label each flowerpot with a number from 1 to 10. Provide two pairs of child-sized gardening gloves, two gardening hats, two aprons (optional), and 55 artificial flowers (available at most craft stores). Have a pair of students wear the hats, aprons, and gloves and "plant" the correct number of flowers in each flowerpot by pushing the stems into the floral foam. Encourage students to count aloud as they "plant" the flowers.

Counting Flower "Seeds"

Materials: Flower Pattern (page 107), yellow paper, marker, scissors, small container, large dried beans, write-on/wipe-away markers

Make 10 enlarged copies of the Flower Pattern on yellow paper. On each pattern, write a number from 1 to 10 for each student to trace. (If desired, write the numbers with dotted lines.) Cut out and laminate the patterns for durability. Supply a container of large dried beans to represent flower seeds. Let students use write-on/wipe-away markers to trace each number and then count the matching number of "seeds" to place on the flower.

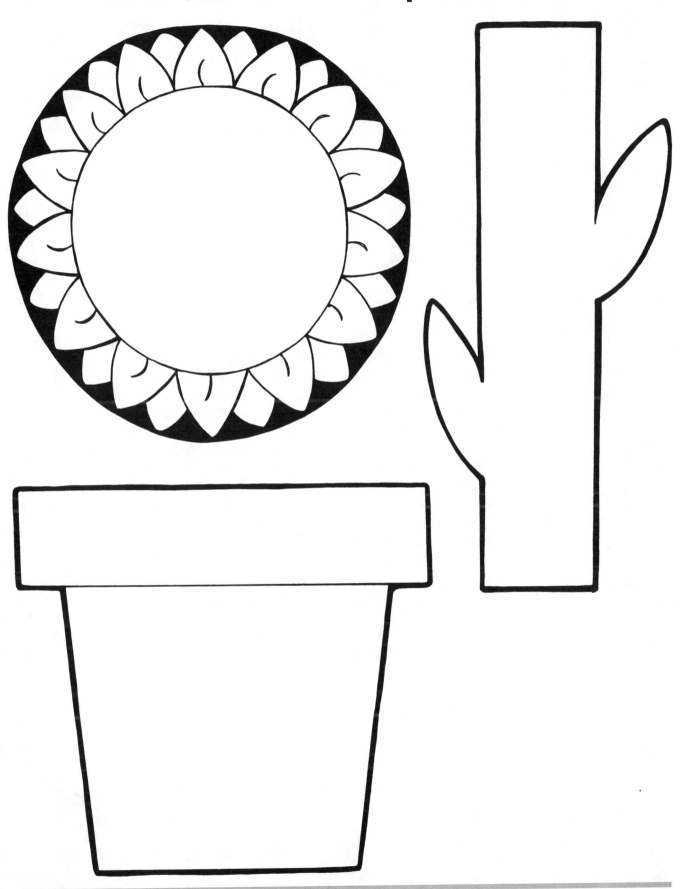

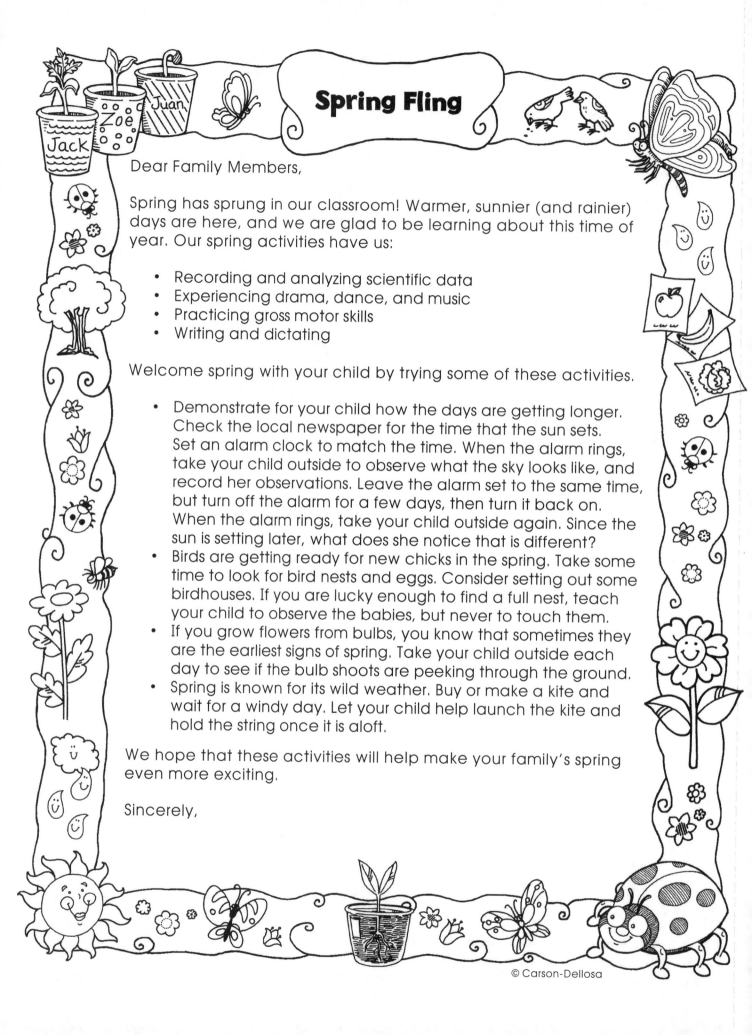

Spring Fling

Dear Family Members,

Spring has sprung in our classroom! Warmer, sunnier (and rainier) days are here, and we are glad to be learning about this time of year. Our spring activities have us:

- Recording and analyzing scientific data
- Experiencing drama, dance, and music
- Practicing gross motor skills
- Writing and dictating

Welcome spring with your child by trying some of these activities.

- Demonstrate for your child how the days are getting longer. Check the local newspaper for the time that the sun sets. Set an alarm clock to match the time. When the alarm rings, take your child outside to observe what the sky looks like, and record her observations. Leave the alarm set to the same time, but turn off the alarm for a few days, then turn it back on. When the alarm rings, take your child outside again. Since the sun is setting later, what does she notice that is different?
- Birds are getting ready for new chicks in the spring. Take some time to look for bird nests and eggs. Consider setting out some birdhouses. If you are lucky enough to find a full nest, teach your child to observe the babies, but never to touch them.
- If you grow flowers from bulbs, you know that sometimes they are the earliest signs of spring. Take your child outside each day to see if the bulb shoots are peeking through the ground.
- Spring is known for its wild weather. Buy or make a kite and wait for a windy day. Let your child help launch the kite and hold the string once it is aloft.

We hope that these activities will help make your family's spring even more exciting.

Sincerely,

Students look forward to summer all year long. For some students it means days off from school or child care. To others, it means trips to the pool or the beach or to visit family. It means wearing shorts, eating frozen treats, staying up later, catching fireflies, and reading plenty of books. Whether your class takes a break, you can tap into some of those wonderful experiences with a summer unit. Use summer fun to help students practice other skills, such as experimenting with light and making shape art; enjoying special summer treats such as ice cream, lemonade, and watermelon; role-playing; and doing math activities with watermelon seeds.

Literature Selections

Come On, Rain! by Karen Hesse (Scholastic, 1999). Hesse perfectly captures the renewing bliss of a summer downpour after a long, hot, miserable stretch of days.

Higher! Higher! by Leslie Patricelli (Candlewick Press, 2009). This uniquely colorful book is about a dreamy girl who swings higher and higher into the sky, and flies over rooftops, mountains, and airplanes. Illustrations are acrylic on canvas, which creates an especially vivid effect.

How I Spent My Summer Vacation by Mark Teague (Dragonfly Books, 1997). Instead of reading the usual essay about what he did over the summer vacation, Wallace Bleff treats his classmates to a tall tale of his rollicking adventures out west.

One Hot Summer Day by Nina Crews (Greenwillow Books, 1995). Somehow, summer seems hotter in the city, especially as described by this young narrator.

Summer by Alice Low (Random House Books for Young Readers, 2001). Crammed with all of the things that make summer special, this book will make you long for summer—especially if read in the middle of winter.

Summer Stinks by Marty Kelley (Zino Press Children's Books, 2001). A funny rhyming alphabet book about all of the reasons why summer is not so terrific, after all. Students will giggle at the grouchy narrator.

Sunshine Fade Art

Materials: construction paper, scissors, tape

Cut out a variety of shapes from construction paper. Place the supplies on a table. Students should use small pieces of tape to attach a variety of precut shapes to a whole sheet of construction paper. When the pieces of artwork are complete, have students tape their artwork to a window that receives plenty of direct sunlight. The artwork should be facing toward the outside. After one week, let students remove the art from the windows. Each student should carefully remove the shapes from her artwork to observe the changes. Ask students why they think that the construction paper looks different. What do they think caused the changes?

Beach Ball Bounce

Materials: small, inflatable beach balls; tennis rackets; beach music

Inflate the beach balls. Clear plenty of room for this activity. Let students practice bouncing the beach balls on the rackets. Then, play the music and let them bounce the beach balls to the beat of the music. Depending on students' abilities, allow them to dribble the beach balls instead of using the rackets. Encourage students to dance to the music whenever they need a break from bouncing the beach balls.

Attracting the Sun

Materials: construction paper in black, white, and 3 other colors; scissors; envelopes; chocolate chips; resealable plastic bags; warm, sunny place outside or gooseneck lamps with high-wattage bulbs; pencils and crayons

Cut the construction paper into strips, each approximately 2" × 3" (5 cm × 7.5 cm). Place one strip of each color in an envelope for each student. Place five chocolate chips in a resealable plastic bag for each student. Students can conduct this experiment outside if it is a hot, sunny day, or they can do it under warm lamps inside. If using lamps, place them on a table, plug them in, and turn them on so that they can heat up. Place the rest of the supplies on the table in the center. Each student should remove her strips of paper from the envelope and align them in a row on the ground in the sun or on the table under the lamps. She should then place one chocolate chip on top of each strip of paper. If using lamps, bend the necks of the lamps so that the bulbs are close to the surface of the table without touching it. While waiting for the results, have each student draw a small circle of each color on a piece of paper to match each of the strips in the experiment. Tell students to observe the chocolate chips to see which one begins to melt first. Which color paper caused the chocolate chip to melt first? Which started to melt last? Have students draw a circle around the color that caused melting to start first and an X over the color that caused melting to start last. Let students discuss their findings.

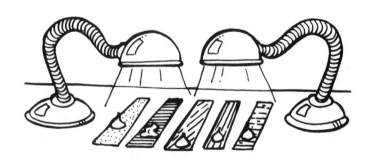

 **(See page 2.)**

Summer Fun

Dear Family Members,

Long, lazy days and warm, hazy nights—it is summertime in our classroom and your children are having fun in the sun. Along with their sun-drenched activities, your children are acquiring new skills and obtaining additional practice in important areas, such as:

- Observing, recording, and analyzing scientific data
- Preparing and eating healthy foods
- Moving to and appreciating music
- Counting and graphing
- Using fine motor skills with art materials

Stretch your child's summertime fun with these activities.

- Summer reading is a great way to bond with your child. Go to a library, bookstore, or book Web site with your child. Let him browse through the books and list all of the books that he wants to read over the summer. Post the list in his room. Purchase or borrow a few at a time. Each time he reads a book on the list, put a star next to the book. When he finishes his summer reading list, reward him with a treat.
- Summertime is a great time for bathing your dog outside. Let your child help pamper your pooch. Make sure that the dog is secured in a tub or on a leash, and supervise closely. If possible, use environmentally-friendly dog shampoo.
- Play in the sprinkler or wash the car together.
- If you live in a neighborhood with an ice cream truck, let your child enjoy a frozen treat. Store a small amount of ice cream money in an easy-to-reach place.

These activities will keep the special feeling of summer alive all year long.

Sincerely,

What's the Weather?

Students love splashing in puddles, basking in the sun, and racing downhill on their sleds. Since weather affects outdoor play, seasonal clothing, and even their school schedule, students are always interested in learning about the weather. As you teach students about different types of weather, work in learning activities, such as creating unusual art projects, role playing in a weather station, scientific weather observation, and enjoying songs and rhymes about weather. Incorporate literature by reading *The Cloud Book* and *It Looked Like Spilt Milk* before embarking on a cloud-watching session. Combine the weather station dramatic play area with a reading of *Weather Words and What they Mean*. And for a fun class snack, sample some pancakes on a rainy morning as you read *Cloudy with a Chance of Meatballs*.

Literature Selections

The Cloud Book by Tomie de Paola (Holiday House, 1984). In easy-to-understand language, this book names the most common types of clouds and what kinds of weather they may bring.

Cloudy With a Chance of Meatballs by Judi Barrett (Aladdin, 1982). Chewandswallow is a marvelous town that feeds all of its residents from the sky, but disaster strikes when the weather changes and the falling food becomes too much of a good thing.

It Looked Like Spilt Milk by Charles G. Shaw (HarperFestival, 1992). This classic book about cloud watching can lead to a cloud-watching session with students.

To Be Like the Sun by Susan Marie Swanson (Harcourt Children's Books, 2008). A little girl's contagious curiosity about each stage in a sunflower's growth will easily engage young students. Each page has brief, lyrical lines of poetry and exuberant illustrations.

Weather Words and What They Mean by Gail Gibbons (Holiday House, 1992). Here is a simple but thorough introduction to weather words and their meanings.

Wind Art

Materials: thinned tempera paint, bowls, paper, shallow box or bin that is at least 9" x 12" (23 cm x 30 cm), plastic spoons, plastic drinking straws

Pour the thinned paints into bowls. Place the supplies on a table. Have a student place one sheet of paper in the bottom of the box. (The edges of the box will keep the paints from splattering.) Tell her to use a spoon to place a small amount of paint on the paper. Then, let each student use her own straw to blow the paint, spreading it across the paper. Caution: Warn students not to suck air *in* through the straw, but only to blow air *out*. Encourage students to experiment by blowing directly over the paint, from side to side, quickly, or softly. When a student completes her wind art, remove it from the box and set it aside to dry.

How Many Snowflakes in a Snowstorm?

Materials: black or dark blue construction paper, white chalk, aerosol hair spray (optional)

Place the supplies on a table. Show students how to draw a snowflake. Remind them that no two snowflakes are alike, so they can draw snowflakes in a variety of ways. Have each student use chalk to draw a snowstorm on his paper. Then, tell him to number the snowflakes on his paper. (Tip: Spray aerosol hair spray on students' papers to keep chalk from smearing.) Encourage students to count aloud the number of snowflakes in their snowstorms.

Storm Dance

Chant this rhyme as you lead students in creating an indoor storm dance.

Storm Dance

The wind picks up…	(wave arms back and forth)
The clouds roll in…	(lie down and roll across the room)
It begins to sprinkle…	(rub fingers together, softly tap toes)
The rain comes down…	(fingers wiggle as hands fall down)
Faster and faster.	(pat knees progressively louder and faster)
A crack of lightning	(one loud clap)
Slices through the sky!	(clap twice and leap side to side)
Thunder rolls…	(stomp feet)
Hail pounds…	(pound or stomp on the floor)
The rain slows, then stops.	(clap progressively softer and slower)
The wind stops blowing…	(slow the breezy movements until very still)
The clouds move on…	(roll across the room)
The sun shines again.	(lie back quietly and sigh)

Make a Rainstorm

While sitting cross-legged in the circle, have students imitate what you do to create the sound of a rainstorm gradually building up and then slowing down again. Discourage students from talking. Encourage them to just listen and imagine that they are making the sounds of a rainstorm. Slowly rub your hands together. Snap your fingers with any students who can snap. The other students should keep rubbing their hands. Then, slap your legs with your hands. Next, stomp your feet and slap your legs at the same time (or alternately). Just slap your legs with your hands. Then, snap your fingers. Then, rub your hands together. Now, stop and listen to the quiet.

Snowy, Cloudy, Rainy, Sunny

Materials: Weather Cards (page 118), scissors, crayons or markers

Enlarge the Weather Cards and cut them apart. Color and laminate them for durability. Teach students the action for each card.

- Snowy: Lift up and down onto tiptoes while floating arms through the air.
- Cloudy: Crouch down into a tight ball.
- Rainy: Hold hands over head as if protecting yourself from rain while running quickly in place.
- Sunny: Hold arms open wide, bend head back as if basking in the sun, and sigh, "Ahhh!"

Place all of the Weather Cards facedown in front of you. Tell students that each time that you say a weather word and show the card, they should act like that weather word as shown above until you show the next card. Very slowly, show one card at a time while students perform the associated activities. Gradually increase the speed of the game by saying the words in random order more and more quickly. See how quickly students can respond before they melt into puddles of giggles and confusion.

All Kinds of Weather

Materials: paper, marker, scissors, balloon

Draw different weather symbols (sun, clouds, raindrops, snowflakes) on sheets of paper. Cut them apart. Talk about each symbol and how it describes a certain type of weather. When the sun is out, what does it feel like? What clothes do we wear? What do we call that kind of day? How do you feel when we have a sunny day? Repeat with the other weather symbols. Decide what kind of day it is today and pin that symbol by the calendar. Put the other symbols nearby so that you can discuss the weather each day. Inflate a balloon in front of students. Ask students what is inside the balloon. They will probably say, "Air." Ask them how they know that there is air in the balloon. They may say that they saw you blow it in the balloon or that the shape of the balloon tells them that there is air in it. Slowly release the air so it blows your hair or something light as evidence that there is air in it. Ask students where else they see evidence of the air around them (flags blowing, leaves moving, sailboat, feel the breeze on their skin, etc.).

 **(See page 2.)**

Rainy Environment

Materials: clean, empty food jar; aluminum pie pan; ice; thermos full of boiling water; flashlight (optional)

Make a rainy environment in a jar. Use a clean, empty food jar and an aluminum pie pan full of ice. Pour about one cup of boiling water (from a thermos) into the jar. Quickly cover with the pan full of ice. (If possible, turn out the light and shine a flashlight in the jar.) As you observe the jar, ask students to describe what is happening. You should see the inside of the jar filling with a cloud and drops of water. The bottom of the pan will become heavy with water. Ask students where that water is coming from. Some students will probably think that it is leaking through the lid. (You do not need to introduce the word *condensation*—just provide the experience.) Ask them if they have ever seen anything like this anywhere else, then explain that rain comes from clouds when they cannot hold any more moisture, just like the cloud in the jar.

 **(See page 2.)**

Snow

Recite this poem as you perform the motions with students.

Snow

Snow comes twirling from the sky,	(twirl your body)
Dancing snowflakes flying high.	(dance and twirl)
The sky is filled with gentle lace	(twirl and wiggle fingers around)
Drifting down to find its place.	(wiggle fingers and bring hands down)
In cold white blankets, snowflakes lie.	(move hands back and forth, palms down)

Windy Day

Materials: electric fan, sheet of paper or a plastic grocery bag, Weather Vane Pattern (page 117), wooden dowel or pencil

Using a fan and a sheet of paper or a plastic grocery bag, show students what things look like when they blow in the wind. Create a weather vane using a wooden dowel or a pencil and the Weather Vane Pattern. Show students how a weather vane works. (It always points in the direction that the wind is blowing.) So, if the weather vane is pointing to the right, then the wind is blowing to the right. Stand in front of the class with the weather vane. Tell them that they are going to be blown by the wind, but that they must watch the weather vane to know which way to go. Turn the weather vane in one direction while the class "blows" to one side of the room. Remind them how the fan moved the paper and the plastic bag so that students will move similarly. Now, point the weather vane in the other direction until the entire class has blown to the opposite side of the room. Point the weather vane in a new direction, sending students in that direction. Change the direction of the weather vane mid-romp or spin the weather vane in circles to indicate a swirling wind. Invite students to take turns being the weather vane controller.

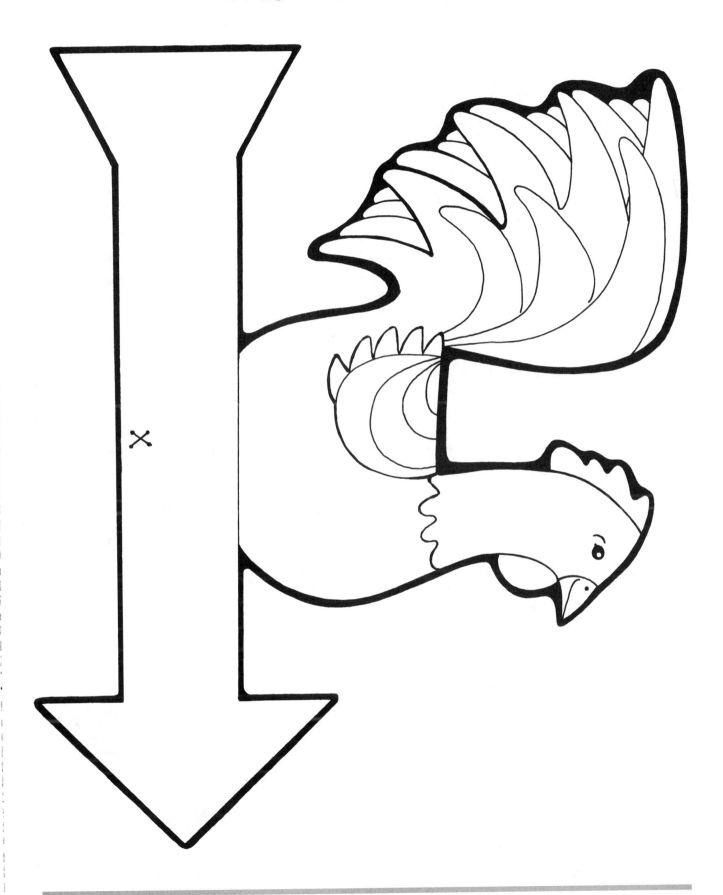

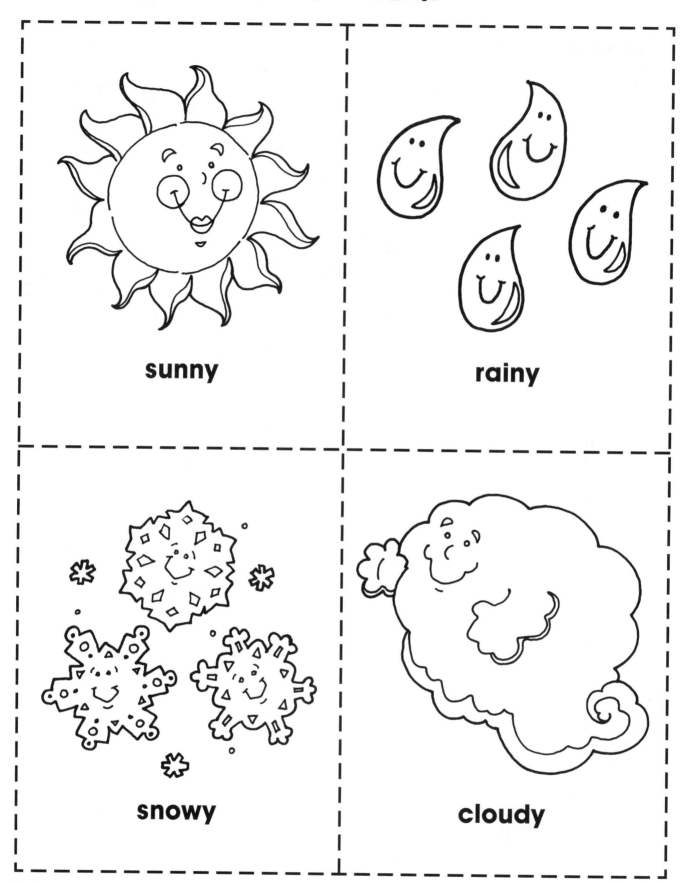

sunny

rainy

snowy

cloudy

What's the Weather?

Dear Family Members,

"What is the weather going to be like?" People always want to know the answer to this question, and children are no exception, since weather can make or break their plans. During our "What's the Weather?" unit, children will learn about:

- Working with technology
- Predicting and discussing scientific concepts
- Exploring weather-related vocabulary
- Performing movement activities

Help your child become a weather-watcher with these activities.

- Watch or listen to a weather forecast with your child, or look at one in a newspaper. Point to recognizable features, such as the letters L and H (low and high pressure systems), rain and sun icons, and numbers (temperature). Explain any words that she does not understand. Talk about the weather forecast. Let her draw a picture of the predicted weather for the next day. In the morning, take a walk outside so that she can see if the forecast was correct.
- It is fun to observe clouds and look for shapes, but you can look for more than that. With your child, observe the differences between low, heavy clouds that bring rain or snow, and puffy clouds that can bring thunderstorms. Help him notice that the clouds are always moving and changing.
- Talk about weather safety with your child. Make sure that she knows what to do during threatening weather. Enlist her help to formulate a safety plan for severe storms.

These activities will help you connect with your child in any weather.

Sincerely,

Transportation Celebration

Airborne airplanes, wailing fire trucks, shiny school buses, noisy motorcycles, enormous excavators, grungy garbage trucks—at some point, many students become captivated by vehicles. Sometimes, it starts with playing with a toy steering wheel or beeping the horn in a parent's car; at other times it starts with a trip to the airport to pick up a visiting relative. There is so much to do in a transportation unit: learn how simple machines work in the car repair shop center, learn how to spot and read road signs by recognizing their shapes and colors, practice classification skills by naming vehicles with wheels, and other easy math, movement, art, and language activities. The literature for this unit can get kids on the move. Sail toy boats in the water table after reading *Little Bear's Little Boat*. Have a class clean-up day as a follow-up to *I Stink!* Go to the playground and let students raise their arms in an in-playground flight as a tribute to *Amazing Airplanes*. And finally, build a hill on your classroom train table so students can reenact *The Little Engine That Could*.

Literature Selections

Amazing Airplanes by Tony Mitton and Ant Parker (Kingfisher, 2005). Rhyming text celebrates airplane parts and the people who keep planes in the air. The book also includes a page that shows the parts of a plane and an airport.

The Grumpy Dump Truck by Brie Spangler (Knopf Books for Young Readers, 2009). When Bertrand, the grouchy dump truck, meets cheerful porcupine construction worker Tilly, Bertrand's attitude begins to change.

I Stink! by Kate McMullan (HarperCollins, 2006). This boisterous, swaggering truck eats garbage for breakfast, and he is proud of it! Students will love this larger-than-life character and the very clear depiction of the piles of trash that he consumes.

Little Bear's Little Boat by Eve Bunting (Clarion Books, 2003). Little Bear loves his little boat. It is his best friend—until he gets too big for it. He gives the boat to another little bear, fulfilling his destiny as well as the boat's. Students will love the idea of owning their own boat.

The Little Engine That Could by Watty Piper (Grosset & Dunlap, 1990). This classic tale about a little engine who "thought she could" still captivates and motivates students today.

The Wheels on the Bus by Paul O. Zelinsky (Dutton Juvenile, 1990). What student does not love "The Wheels on the Bus"? This version combines flaps and pull-tabs with the classic song to add even more interaction and interest.

Who Sank the Boat? by Pamela Allen (Putnam Juvenile, 1996). Four animals climb into a boat, then sink—and swim.

Tire Painting

Materials: tempera paint; large foil roasting pans; large bowl; water; toy vehicles that have wheels (look for tires that have different kinds of treads); paper; towels

Pour a thin layer of paint in the bottom of each roasting pan. Fill a large bowl half full of water. Place the supplies on a table. Let each student choose a toy vehicle and roll it gently in a tray of paint to coat the wheels. Then, tell him to "drive" the toy over his paper in any direction that he chooses. (Remind students not to press too hard so that the tires will leave patterns on their papers.) Students can coat the tires with the same color paint again, dip the toy in the bowl of water to rinse off the residue and use a different paint color, or switch to a different toy. When students are finished, set aside the paintings to dry. Have students help wash all of the vehicles and dry them with towels.

Car Repair Shop

Materials: small ride-on toys, such as cars, tricycles, bicycles with training wheels, or wagons; toy tools; empty, clean plastic bottles; short garden hoses; skateboard; buckets; rags; towels; sponges; handheld vacuum; toy cash register; money manipulatives; chairs; magazines; paper; crayons or markers

Create a car repair shop and car wash area for the ride-on toys. Make a garage area with tools, plastic bottles (for "oil" and other "fluids"), hoses (for "air" and "water"), and a skateboard or wheeled sled for mechanics to use while working on the lower parts of the vehicles (secure long hair to prevent a snag in the wheels). Establish a car wash area with hoses, buckets, rags, towels, sponges, and a handheld vacuum. Place the cash register and money manipulatives on a table to represent the checkout area. Nearby, place the chairs and magazines in a customer waiting area. Also, place the paper and crayons or markers in this area so that customers can create their own personalized license plates while they wait. (Visit official state and province Web sites to find sample images of license plates to print and display for students.) Help students decide who will play each role. They will need at least one mechanic, a cashier, several car wash technicians, and customers. Mechanics will need jumpsuits or overalls to protect their clothing. Encourage the customers to bring their vehicles for service and then describe and demonstrate the funny sounds and other problems that they need fixed. Have the mechanics repair the vehicles and let the cashiers assist the customers in designing personalized license plates.

Vamoose Caboose!

Divide students into teams of three and have each team form a single file line. Have each child hold on to the waist of the child in front of him to create a train. At your signal, have each "train" leave the "station" across the "track." As the engine picks up steam, have the first child pump her arms faster and faster. Explain that as the engine winds and turns its way along the track, chances are that she might lose the caboose. If the caboose (the child at the back of the train) lets go or gets lost, he must quickly find another train of students to join. After a few minutes, stop and have the team members switch so that everyone gets a chance to be an engine and a caboose.

Variation: As the trains chug around the play area, have them listen for the train whistle. When they hear the signal, all of the cabooses should separate and scramble to find other trains to join.

Wheels or No Wheels?

Materials: index cards, Transportation Cards (page 127), scissors

Ask students to think of things that have wheels. Write all of the things that they name on index cards. Sort the cards into meaningful categories: wheels under our feet, wheels without motors, four wheels. Talk about the fact that wheels help us move faster. Think of other ways that we get around without wheels (or with wheels that are just for landing and taking off). Pose different questions about the best way to get to someone's house. For example, what is the best way to get to your grandma's house? For some students, it may be by car, while for others it may be by plane or by foot. Discuss the reasons for the different answers. Ask students to think about the speed of transportation. Duplicate the Transportation Cards. Cut apart the cards. Put the cards in order from slowest to fastest.

Parking Garage

Materials: old shoe box, scissors, number cards, toy cars

Decorate an old shoe box to look like a garage. Cut doors in the side for cars to drive in. Put a number card on the garage. Allow students to take turns driving the correct number of toy cars into the garage. Change the number card so that students can practice counting to different numbers as they drive cars in and out.

1 Honk, 2 Honks, 3 Honks

Materials: premade audio tape, tape player, masking tape

Prepare a tape by recording the sound of a car honking once, twice, or three times in a row. Leave approximately 10 seconds between each series of honks. Use masking tape to create three large squares on the floor. Inside each square, tape a number 1, 2, or 3. Place the tape player and premade tape on a table. Instruct students to start the tape and listen for the car honks. Tell them to count the number of honks that they hear and then go to the corresponding square. Encourage them to move from square to square as if they are operating a variety of vehicles, such as a fast car, a huge truck, a boat, or an airplane.

Pass the Car

Materials: toy car

Have students sit in a circle on the floor. Choose one student to sit in the center of the circle with his eyes closed. The center student should say, "Green light," to make the other students pass a car around the circle behind their backs. When the student in the center says, "Red light," the person with the car must hold it. All students should keep their hands behind their backs. The center student may open his eyes and try three times to guess who is holding the car. The student who is holding the car goes in the center next.

Mystery Sort

Materials: a variety of toy vehicles

Think of a category for sorting vehicles, but do not tell the class. For example, you could sort into categories of blue vehicles, no wheels, or construction vehicles. Put all of the vehicles that fit your category in the center of the circle. Ask students to guess what your sorting rule is.

Number Trains

Materials: Train Engine and Train Car Patterns (page 129), colorful paper, scissors, markers, stickers, stamps, ink pads with washable ink

Make 10 enlarged copies of the Train Engine Pattern on colorful paper and cut out the patterns. Label each engine with a number from 1 to 10. Laminate the engines for durability. Enlarge and make 10 copies of the Train Car Pattern for each student. Post a numbered train engine on a bulletin board. Give each student a train car to cut out. Then, provide stickers and stamps and ink pads or markers and have students create sets to match the number shown on the train engine. As students complete their train cars, let them attach the cars to the engine to create a number train. Create more number trains with the remaining engines.

Take Your Seats

Materials: classroom chairs, paper, markers

Create a classroom bus station, complete with a driver and tickets. Make two rows of chairs equal to the total number of students in the class, with an aisle in between. Label the chairs in sequential order by attaching numbered sheets of paper to the backs of the chairs. (If students only know numbers from 1 to 10 and there are more than 10 students in the class, divide the chairs into two rows and label two sets of chairs from 1 to 10.) Pretend to be a bus driver and give each student a "bus ticket" (a sheet of paper with a number written on it). To board the bus, students should form a line and hand you their tickets. Use a hole punch to "check in" each "passenger" and let him find his seat on the bus by matching the number on his ticket to the number on a chair. After all of the students have found their seats, have them count by reading aloud the numbers on their tickets.

Up, Up, and Away!

Materials: Hot Air Balloon Pattern (page 130), colorful (solid or patterned) paper, scissors, yarn or string, clothespins or paper clips

Enlarge and make a supply of the Hot Air Balloon Pattern on colorful patterned or solid paper. Cut out the balloons. Attach a piece of yarn or string across a bulletin board at students' eye level. Using clothespins or paper clips, attach three or four balloons to the yarn in a pattern. Let students finish the pattern. Students can also create patterns for each other.

Navigating the Numbers

Materials: paper, marker, masking tape, variety of toy vehicles

Write numbers from 1 to 10 on sheets of paper. Scatter the sheets of paper randomly on the floor and tape them securely in place. Make "roads" between the numbers by stretching pieces of masking tape from number to number in order. Have each student choose a toy vehicle and find the number 1 on the floor. Tell students to travel along the number roads by driving, flying, or steering their vehicles from 1 to 10. Encourage them to make noises like their vehicles and count aloud as they reach each number. For a challenge, have students travel backward from 10 to 1.

Parade of Cars

Materials: Car Pattern (page 129), colorful paper, scissors, pencils

Enlarge and make one copy of the Car Pattern on colorful paper for each student. Give each student a pattern to cut out. Assign each student a number and let her write it on her car. Help students as needed. (If students only know numbers from 1 to 10 and there are more than 10 students in the class, divide the class into two groups and let each group make numbered cars from 1 to 10.) Have students sit in a large circle and slowly count aloud together. As each number is called, the student (or students) with that numbered car should create a line of cars in the middle of the circle. By the time students have counted to 10, the class will have created a parade of cars in numerical order.

Transportation Identification

Materials: a variety of transportation toys or pictures of vehicles, magazines, scissors, index cards, glue

Gather a variety of transportation toys, such as trucks, cars, boats, airplanes, construction vehicles, and community service vehicles. If toys are not readily available, find pictures of modes of transportation in magazines, cut them out, and glue them to index cards. Laminate the transportation cards for durability. Have students sort the modes of transportation in a variety of ways, such as whether the vehicles travel by land, sea, or air; how they are used (for rescue, for construction, for taking people to work); by size; or by the number of passengers that they hold.

Sailing into Math

Materials: Sailboat Pattern (page 130), colorful paper, markers, scissors

Create a math problem matching game for students to practice math facts. Copy a supply of the Sailboat Pattern on colorful paper. Write addition and subtraction facts on some of the sailboats. Write the answers to the facts on the remaining sailboats. Cut out and laminate the sailboats for durability. Let students match the problems with the correct answers. Students can work with partners or complete this activity independently.

Road Race

Materials: tape, index cards, toy car, Number Cube Pattern (page 128), card stock

Make roads by taping index cards together end to end, alternating plain white with lined cards or alternating colors so that the cards can be easily counted. Provide one road and a toy car for each student. Copy one Number Cube Pattern on card stock for each pair of students. On each cube pattern, label the squares with different numbers from 1 to 10. Assemble the cubes by folding along the small dotted lines and taping the edges. Select two students to be partners. Have partners place their roads side by side on the floor or a table. Have players take turns rolling the number cube and "driving" their cars over that number of index cards on the road. The first player to reach the end of his road wins. Players then return to their starting lines and begin again.

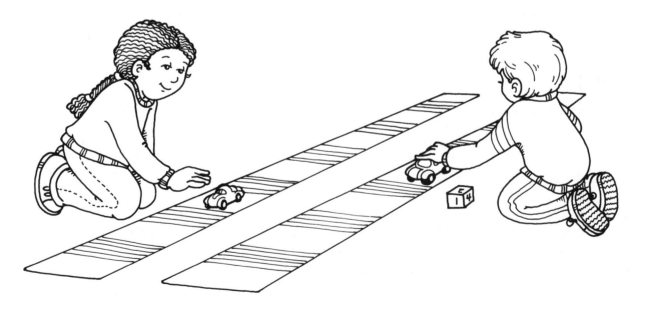

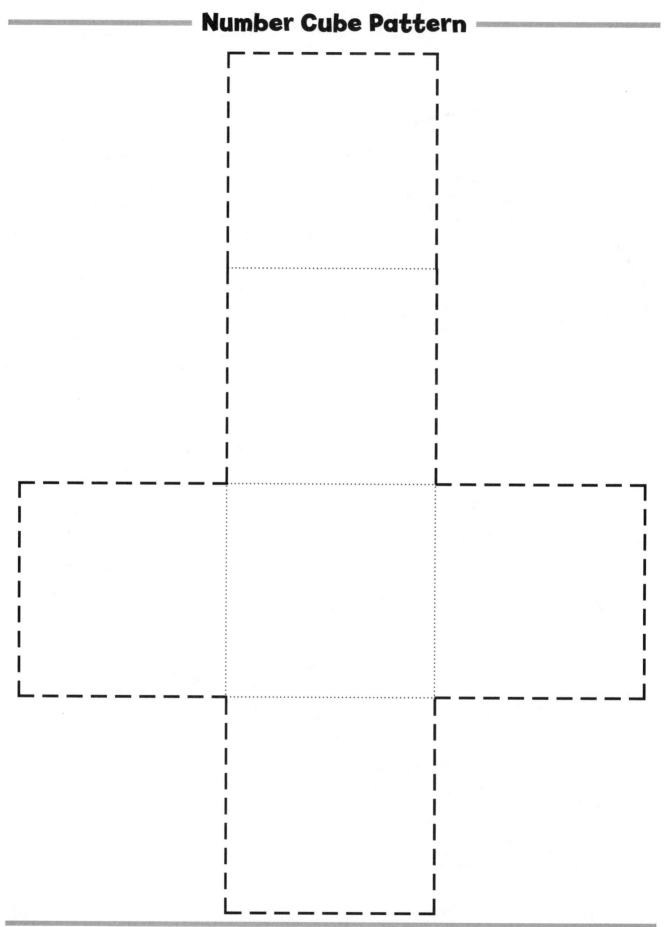

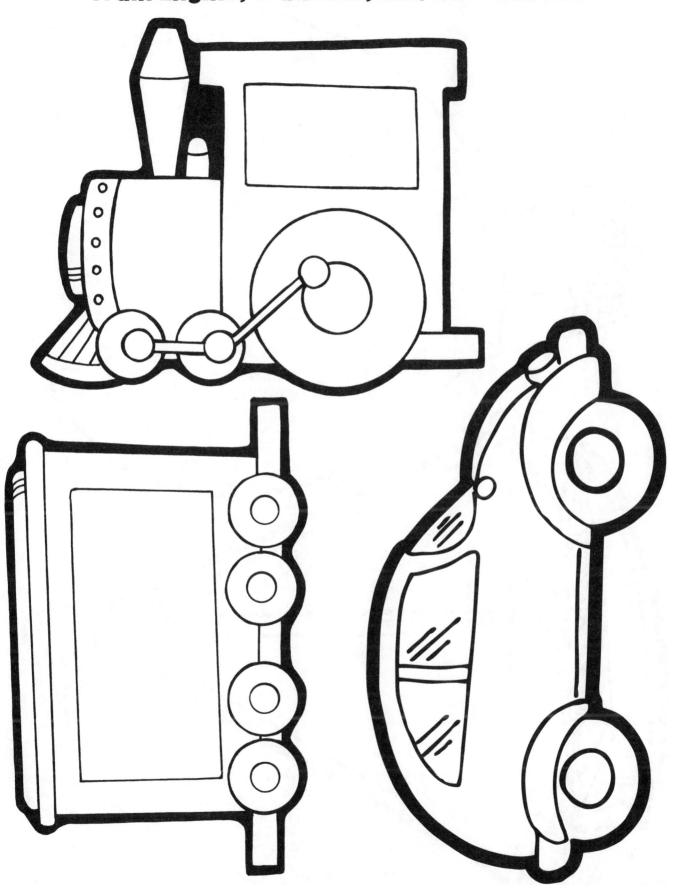

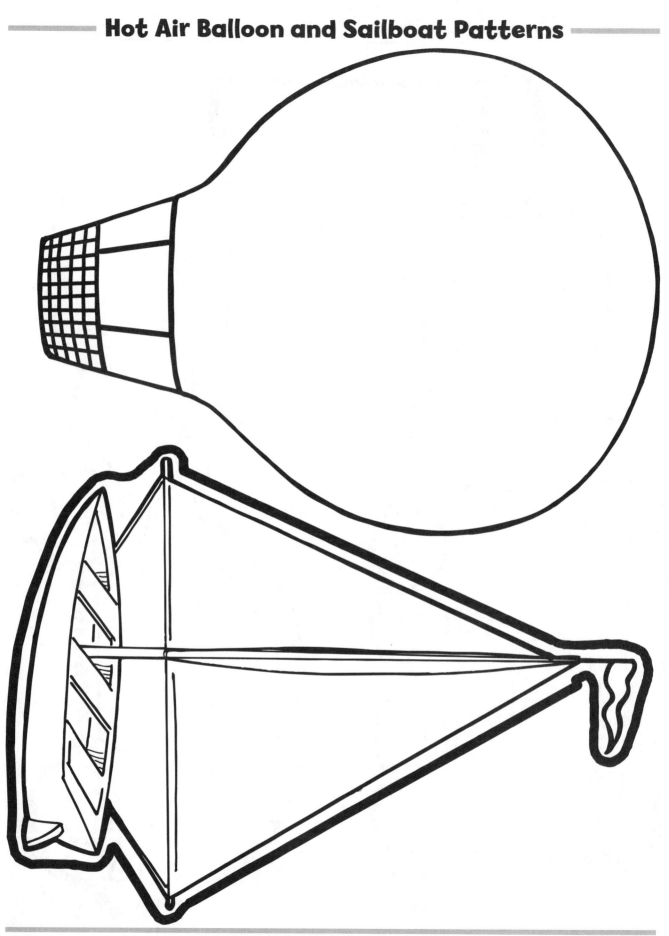

Transportation Celebration

Dear Family Members,

We are on the go with our "Transportation Celebration" unit. We are exploring cars, boats, trains, and planes. We have combined all of these fun activities with other skill-based activities, such as:

- Predicting outcomes and recording scientific data
- Improving gross motor skills
- Preparing healthy foods
- Participating in dramatic play
- Learning rhymes and songs

Drive home the learning with these fun activities.

- While outside with your child, look for airplanes and contrails—frozen water vapor trails that planes leave in the sky.
- Many young children love school buses. Their unusual shape, huge size, and bright color make them very appealing. If you have a bus that stops in your neighborhood, make a point to go outside when it arrives. Help your child read the school bus's numbers, read the letters on the side of the bus, or count the tires and windows.
- Take your child to a high floor in a tall building and let her look out the window. Have her look down to see the vehicles below. Have her identify trucks and cars. Discuss why the vehicles look so small.
- If you do not have a train set, make a shoe box train. Punch one hole in each short side. Connect the boxes by threading string through the holes and tying it at the top. If you have a red shoe box, be sure to place it at the end for the caboose. Let your child decorate the train, and then drive it around the house.

Have fun transporting your child into a land of fun!

Sincerely,

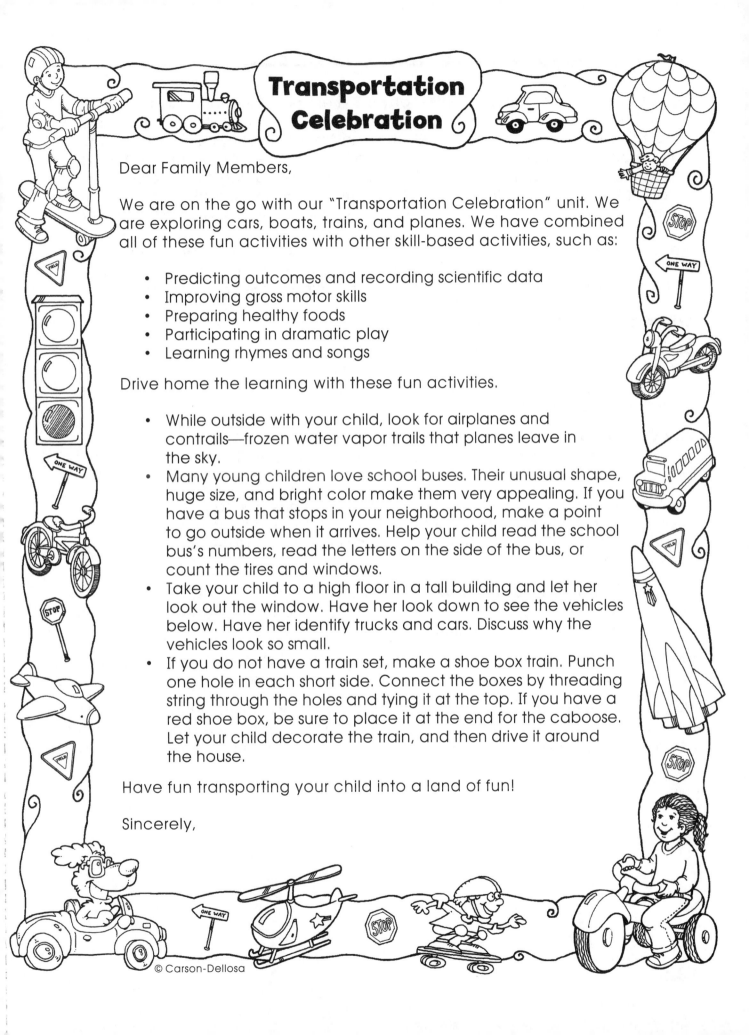

Let's Join the Circus!

One of the first memorable events many children may experience is a trip to the circus. There are so many things for children to love: exotic animals performing tricks, clowns playing jokes on each other, and performers flying through the air or walking on a high-wire. A visit to the big top is sure to be memorable, especially through the eyes of a small child. Bring the excitement of the circus to your classroom by letting children count elephants and peanuts, making math activities special with "rings," and letting children clown around with shape art. All of the literature selections are perfect for inspiring dramatic play. After reading some of the selections, let each child in the classroom choose a type of performer to role-play. Mark three rings on the floor using masking tape, and let performers use dress-up clothing and props as they take turns performing in their own circus.

Literature Selections

Circus by Lois Ehlert (HarperCollins, 1992). Ehlert's classic cut-paper collages make circus performers like the Flying Zucchinis and the Pretzel Brothers seem larger than life. Readers are asked to take a seat at the start of the show as the performers parade across the pages.

The Circus Ship by Chris Van Dusen (Candlewick Press, 2009). After their steamship is wrecked in a storm, a troop of circus animals find safety off the coast of Maine, and win over the wary townspeople with their kind, courageous ways.

If I Ran the Circus by Dr. Seuss (Random House Books for Young Readers, 1956). In Dr. Seuss style, a young boy observes a vacant lot and imagines the most amazing circus in the world. This book is certain to give children ideas for circus role-playing.

Last Night I Dreamed a Circus by Maya Gottfried (Knopf Books for Young Readers, 2003). Easy text and vivid, imaginative pictures take readers through a child's dream about participating in a circus.

See the Circus by H. A. Rey (Houghton Mifflin, 1998). Curious George author H. A. Rey offers an enticing lift-the-flap book that shows all of the goings-on at the circus.

You See a Circus, I See... by Mike Downs (Charlesbridge Publishing, 2006). Meet the narrator's extended family members who just happen to be a group of circus performers. This book is a delight for every child who has imagined running away to the circus.

The Right Number of Peanuts

Materials: Elephant Patterns (page 135), sentence strips, glue, marker, container of packing peanuts or uncooked lima beans

Reduce and copy 55 Elephant Patterns. Glue sets of elephants (from 1 to 10) to 10 sentence strips. If desired, number the elephants on each sentence strip. Provide a container of packing peanuts or uncooked lima beans. Have a student choose a sentence strip set, place it on a table, and "feed" each elephant one "peanut" by placing a peanut on each elephant. Have the student count aloud the number of elephants and the number of peanuts in the set before moving on to the next set.

Elephant-astic Counting

Materials: Elephant Patterns (page 135), scissors, marker, glue, cups or small containers, packing peanuts or uncooked lima beans

Copy and cut out 11 reduced copies of the Elephant Pattern. Label each elephant with a number from 0 to 10. Laminate the elephants for durability. Attach each

elephant to a cup or small container. Have a small group of students sit in a row with the elephant cups in front of them. Provide a bag of packing peanuts or uncooked lima beans for students to use as counters. Allow students to take turns counting and "feeding" each elephant the correct number of "peanuts." When all of the cups contain the correct number of peanuts, have students pour the peanuts into the bag for another group of students to play.

Two-Ring Circus

Materials: large plastic hoops

Place two large, plastic hoops on the floor. Ask two students to hop inside one hoop and three students to hop inside the other hoop. Ask the rest of the class to decide which hoop has more students and which has fewer. Continue playing by having different numbers of students hop in and out of the hoops to create different groups for comparison.

Clowning Around

Materials: colorful paper, scissors, white paper, glue sticks, masking tape, wooden craft sticks

Allow students to use their creativity to make clown shape faces. Cut out a supply of circles, rectangles, squares, and triangles in various sizes and colors. Cut out large, white circles for students to use for their clowns' faces. Place the shapes and several glue sticks on a table. Have students make their own unique clown faces by gluing the shapes in different combinations to create facial features, hair, hats, bow ties, and other decorations. Provide wooden craft sticks for students to tape to the backs of their clowns to make puppets.

Who Spilled the Popcorn?

Materials: 2 small popcorn containers, spinner, marker, timer, bowl, packing peanuts or uncooked lima beans

Gather 2 small popcorn containers (available at party supply stores or the refreshments counter at a movie theater). Label the sections of the spinner *0, 1, 2, 3, 4,* and *Spill the popcorn!* Place all of the supplies on a table. Have students play this game in pairs. Give each student a popcorn container and set the timer for five minutes. Players should take turns spinning the spinner. If it lands on a number greater than zero, the player takes that many pieces of "popcorn" from the bowl and puts them in his container. If the spinner lands on *Spill the popcorn!*, he must pour his popcorn into the bowl. The student with the most popcorn in his popcorn container wins.

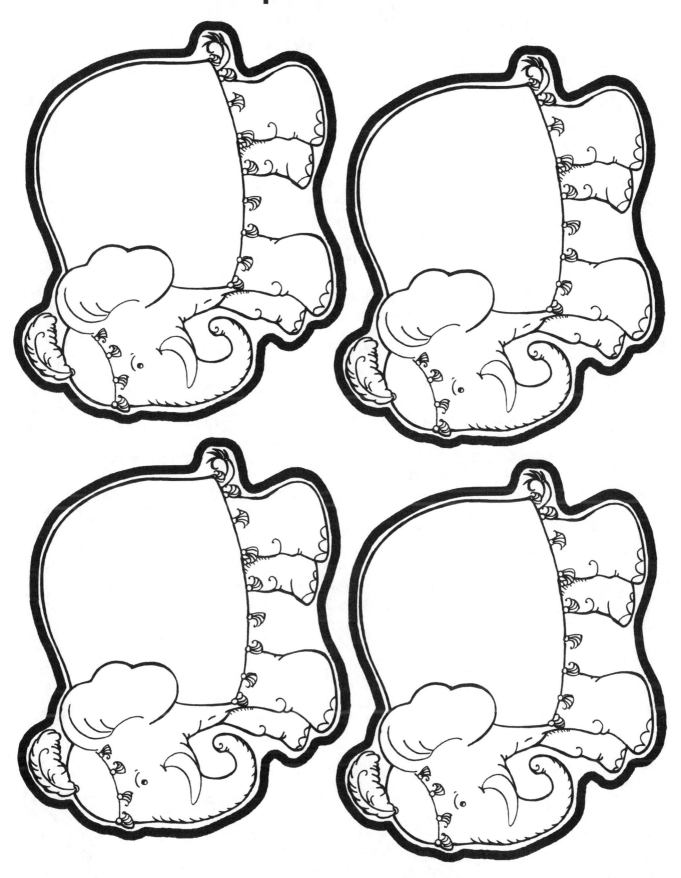

Let's Join the Circus!

Dear Family Members,

Our class is under the big top! We are enjoying plenty of three-ring fun as we learn about the circus. Your children are receiving additional learning opportunities, such as:

- Understanding concepts like *more* and *less*
- Working with shapes
- Counting with manipulatives
- Participating in cooperative games

Use these activities to inspire fun under the big top at home.

- Discuss how lion and tiger "tamers" are actually trainers who teach animals to perform tricks. If you have a dog, see if you and your child can teach him a new trick. Be sure to read about how to train dogs before you start.
- Encourage dramatic play by painting your child's face to look like a clown's face.
- Teach your child a classic, funny clown trick. Fill a plastic cup with paper scraps shredded into confetti. Choose a friend who is a good sport. Let your child pretend to drink from the cup and then dump the "water" on the unsuspecting friend's head.
- Explain that tightrope walkers are masters of balance, and that they often work without a net. Stretch a length of rope along the floor or ground and let your child pretend to walk the tightrope.

Enjoy your circus celebration with your child!

Sincerely,

It's Nursery Rhyme Time!

Nursery rhymes are a ready-made way to help students practice rhyming and word families, as well as other early literacy skills. Students love them because they are silly and funny. And, perhaps the best thing about nursery rhymes is that many teachers (and often students) already have several rhymes memorized. Nursery rhymes are a great jumping-off point for other types of activities, such as counting and telling time with mice, graphing shoes, and learning some new rhymes that would make even Mother Goose proud. Use the literature to lead students into sessions of dramatic play. Let them wear pajamas to school and pretend to stay up late as one student plays Wee Willie Winkie and catches them out of bed. Let them make Jack and Jill figures from cardboard blocks, then tumble them off of a chair (the hill). Or, let students pretend to be mice running up and down the clock as you ring a bell to make the clock "strike one."

Literature Selections

Baa Baa Black Sheep by Iza Trapani (Charlesbridge Publishing, 2001). Everybody wants something from Ms. Black Sheep. She cannot fulfill their original requests, but she happily knits something for each of them, teaching them a lesson about sharing and kindness.

Classic Nursery Rhymes by Paige Weber (Gramercy, 2006). Detailed, rich illustrations show a host of nursery rhymes and popular children's songs.

The Completed Hickory Dickory Dock by Jim Aylesworth (Aladdin, 1994). In the extended version of this rhyme, the mouse does not stop at running up and down the clock. Aylesworth adds additional verses with rhymes that rival the original.

Jack and Jill by Salley Mavor (Houghton Mifflin, 2006). Illustrations of characters created from fabric give these books a unique look. Students will enjoy looking for all of the extra details.

Wee Willie Winkie by Salley Mavor (Houghton Mifflin, 2006). Wee Willie rushes through the town to make sure that children are in bed at the proper time. Students delight in imagining this character who checks to see if they have gone to bed as they should.

The Rain

Teach students the finger play as you recite this poem.

The Rain

Rain on the green grass,	(flutter fingers by the ground)
And rain on the tree,	(stand up straight with arms like branches)
And rain on the housetop,	(hands form point of a roof)
But not on me!	(point at yourself and pretend to raise an umbrella)

One, Two, Buckle My Shoe

Materials: chart paper, marker, 10 index cards, hook-and-loop tape

On a sheet of chart paper, copy the nursery rhyme below, leaving blanks next to the number words. Label 10 index cards with numbers from 1 to 10. Laminate the cards and chart paper for durability. Attach hook-and-loop tape to the chart paper above each blank and to the backs of the cards. Recite the rhyme aloud as a class and have students take turns attaching the correct cards to fill in the blanks on the paper.

One, Two, Buckle My Shoe

One _____ , two _____ , buckle my shoe;

Three _____ , four _____ , shut the door;

Five _____ , six _____ , pick up sticks;

Seven _____ , eight _____ , lay them straight;

Nine _____ , ten _____ , a big red hen.

Hickory, Dickory, Dock

Materials: Clock Pattern (page 142), card stock, scissors, paper fastener, marker, chart paper

Help students practice telling time to the hour with this familiar rhyme. Make an enlarged copy of the Clock Pattern on card stock. Cut out the pieces and laminate them for durability. Use a paper fastener to attach the clock hands to the clock face. Copy the nursery rhyme below on a sheet of chart paper and display it for the class. Set the clock hands to show a time on the hour. Recite the nursery rhyme aloud as a class and have students fill in the time displayed on the clock when they get to the blank. Change the hour shown on the clock each time the class says the rhyme.

Hickory, Dickory, Dock

Hickory, dickory, dock!

The mouse ran up the clock;

The clock struck _____ ,

The mouse ran down,

Hickory, dickory, dock!

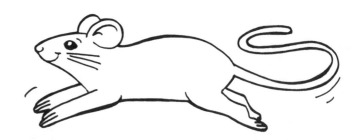

Three-Bear Sort

Materials: *Goldilocks and the Three Bears* (Putnam Juvenile, 1996), Goldilocks and the Three Bears Cards (page 143), scissors, markers, poster board, hook-and-loop tape

Read *Goldilocks and the Three Bears* to students and emphasize the concepts of *small*, *medium*, and *large* found in the story. Make enlarged copies of the Goldilocks and the Three Bears Cards. Cut apart the cards and laminate them for durability. Draw three simple house outlines (small, medium, and large) on a piece of poster board. Attach hook-and-loop tape to the backs of the cards and to the fronts of the houses. Let pairs of students take turns sorting the cards by size or type and attaching them to the poster board. Encourage students to use the cards to make patterns for each other to continue as well.

Hickory, Dickory, Dock

Teach students the finger play to go with this rhyme.

Hickory Dickory, Dock

Hickory, dickory, dock!	(make fists with thumbs up)
The mouse ran up the clock;	(run fingers up arm)
The clock struck one,	(raise one finger)
The mouse ran down,	(run fingers down arm)
Hickory, dickory, dock!	(make fists with thumbs up)

Penguin Limerick

Recite this poem with students.

Days of the Week

There once was a penguin who could speak.
He knew all the days of the week.
He said them of course,
Until he was hoarse.
Now all he can make is a squeak.

Old Mother Hubbard

Students can add their own suggestions to the foods that Mother Hubbard buys and the silly things that the dog does. Illustrate and compile their suggestions into a class book.

Old Mother Hubbard

Old Mother Hubbard went to the cupboard,   (open cupboard doors)
To fetch her poor dog a bone;   (begging hands)
But when she got there,
The cupboard was bare   (shrug with hands up)
And so the poor dog had none.   (make a zero with fingers)
She went to the dock, to buy him some fish,
But when she got back, he was eating his dish.
She went to the baker's to buy him some bread,
But when she got back, he was lying in bed.
She went to the market to buy him some fruit,
But when she got back, he was eating a boot.
She went to the dairy to buy him some cheese,
But when she got back, he was chasing the bees.

One, Two, Three, Four, Five

Have students say this catchy chant while performing the movements.

One, Two, Three, Four, Five

One, two, three, four, five,   (raise one finger at a time on one hand)
Once I caught a fish alive.   (pretend to hold a fishing pole)
Six, seven, eight, nine, ten,   (raise one finger at a time on the other hand)
But, I let it go again.   (put hands together and wiggle them like a
                                          swimming fish)

Why did I let it go?   (raise hands and shrug shoulders)
Because it bit my finger so!   (raise one finger)
Which finger did it bite?   (wiggle all 10 fingers)
The little one on the right.   (raise and wave pinky finger on right hand)

I Love Baseball

Sing to the tune of "Are You Sleeping?" Divide the class into two parts for a call-and-response format.

I Love Baseball

I love baseball. I love baseball.
Hit that ball. Hit that ball.
Let's play at the ballpark. Let's play at the ballpark.
Baseball game, baseball game.

Watch Our Faces

Students must watch to see if you give the "safe" (arms spread from body) or "out" (make a fist with thumb raised and pointed behind you) sign.

Hit the Ball

Hit the ball.   (pretend to bat)
Run the bases.   (arms make running circles)
Make the call.   (make either the safe or out signal)

And watch our faces.   (students act out the call)

Do Your Duty

Say this rhyme as you perform the motions with students.

Pitcher, Pitcher

Pitcher, pitcher, do your duty.   (pretend to throw ball)
Throw this ball; an American beauty.   (salute)
Pitch it fast and pitch it true.   (snap fingers)
Strike him out 'cause we love you.   (cross arms on chest)

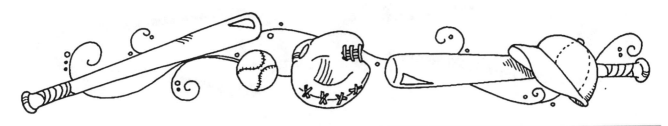

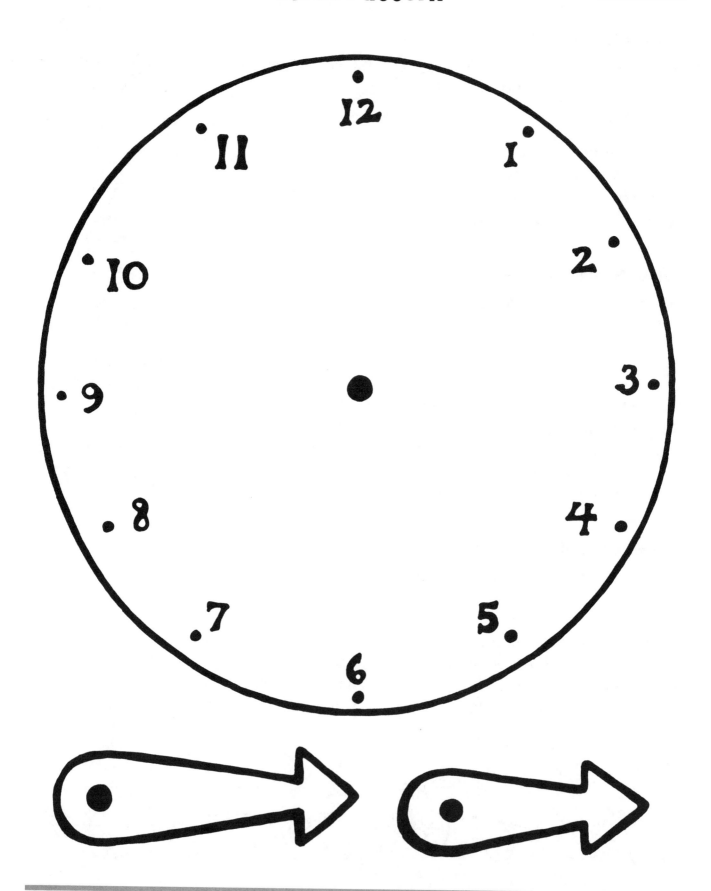

It's Nursery Rhyme Time!

Dear Family Members,

The timeless appeal of nursery rhymes has us over the moon. We are reciting many old favorites and combining them with brand-new skills and activities, like:

- Understanding concepts like *small* and *large*
- Adding finger plays to the rhyming activities
- Working with early math skills like time and picture graphing
- Matching numbers to number words

Make Mother Goose proud with some rhyming fun at home.

- Even after repeating them again and again, children love the surprise of some of the nursery rhyme movements. Teach your child the rhymes and motions for "London Bridge" and "Ring Around the Rosy." Be sure to participate in the actions.
- Give your child a small paper plate, glue, a plastic spoon, and four plastic wiggly eyes. Let him glue the eyes to the plate and spoon to create his own "Hey, Diddle Diddle" puppets.
- If your child can recite many nursery rhymes, play "Name that Rhyme." Supply a couple of words from the beginning of a rhyme as a prompt, and let her say the rest of the rhyme.

Enjoy rhyming and reading with your child!

Sincerely,

Holiday Happenings

Students love to celebrate holidays at school. Even small celebrations are meaningful to students because they make ordinary school days special. This unit includes activities for several popular holidays, including estimating activities for Halloween, playing with Mayflower soap boats for Thanksgiving, making cards for Hanukkah, role-playing with Christmas decorations, making bells to ring in the New Year, creating Valentine's Day art, and searching for the pot of gold in honor of Saint Patrick's Day. Pair each holiday you discuss in class with a literature selection below or with your own tried-and-true holiday book favorites.

Literature Selections

Hurray for Today!: All About Holidays by Bonnie Worth (Random House Books for Young Readers, 2004). This book, from the Dr. Seuss Learning Library, explains all about many different holidays.

Moishe's Miracle: A Hanukkah Story by Laura Krauss Melmed (HarperCollins, 2000). In this new, original tale, generous Moishe gets a special gift on the eve of Hanukkah, but when his wife tries to profit from it, she learns a valuable lesson about love and generosity. The book also includes a summary of the story of Hanukkah.

The Night Before Christmas by Clement C. Moore (HarperCollins, 2004). This classic tale has been illustrated dozens of times, but its charm never fades.

Room for a Little One: A Christmas Tale by Martin Waddell (Margaret K. McElderry, 2006). As an ox welcomes other tired animals into his stable, so he welcomes a tired donkey who happens to be carrying Mary, the mother of Jesus. The animals, in turn, welcome Baby Jesus when he arrives.

Seven Spools of Thread: A Kwanzaa Story by Angela Shelf Medearis (Albert Whitman & Company, 2000). A clever tale of seven arguing brothers and their wise father shares the seven principles of Kwanzaa and also teaches about traditional Kente cloth.

Thanksgiving Is for Giving Thanks by Margaret Sutherland (Grosset & Dunlap, 2000). This book focuses on the variety of things to be thankful for at Thanksgiving.

Trick or Treat? by John Bianchi (Grosset & Dunlap, 2002). This delicious book is dedicated to Halloween's tasty treats.

Decoupage Pumpkins

Materials: small baking pumpkins, permanent marker, colorful tissue paper squares, bowls, glue or liquid starch, foam paintbrushes, disposable plates

Write each student's name on the stem of a pumpkin with a permanent marker. Cut the tissue paper into approximately 1" (2.5 cm) squares. Sort the squares by color and place each color in a different bowl. Thin glue or liquid starch with water and pour it into a bowl. Place all of the supplies on a table. Have each student find the pumpkin with her name on it and place it on a plate. Let each student use a foam paintbrush to apply glue to a small section of the pumpkin. Then, she should stick two or three squares of tissue paper to the glue. Tell her to continue this process until the entire pumpkin is covered in tissue paper. Encourage students to overlap the tissue paper squares to create a colorful stained-glass effect. When the pumpkin is covered, each student should paint a layer of glue over the entire surface to saturate all of the tissue paper. Leave the pumpkins on the plates to dry.

Pumpkin Pie

Near the end of your classroom pumpkin explorations, consider bringing pumpkin pie spice for students to smell or a real pie for them to taste. Sing this song to help students understand how pumpkins go from the patch to pie.

Pumpkin Pie

Pumpkin, pumpkin, I watched you

In my garden as you grew,

From green to orange, what a treat!

Now, as pie, you'll be so sweet.

 **(See page 2.)**

Five Spooky Pumpkins

Materials: pumpkin puppets or felt pumpkins (optional)

After you say the line, perform the actions with students.
This can be used with pumpkin puppets or felt pumpkins.

Five Spooky Pumpkins

Five spooky pumpkins on the stair,	(count on five fingers)
We worked all night for a scare.	(say "Boo")
When the goblins came by	(creep fingers and knock on a door)
Our looks made them shy;	(hide eyes shyly)
Blow out my candle if you dare.	(blow on tip of index finger)
Four spooky pumpkins on the stair,	(count on four fingers)
We worked all night for a scare.	(say "Boo")
When the witches came by	(creep fingers and knock on door)
Our looks made them shy;	(hide eyes shyly)
Blow out my candle if you dare.	(blow on tip of index finger)
Three spooky pumpkins on the stair,	(count on three fingers)
We worked all night for a scare.	(say "Boo")
When the ghosts came by	(creep fingers and knock on door)
Our looks made them shy;	(hide eyes shyly)
Blow out my candle if you dare.	(blow on tip of index finger)
Two spooky pumpkins on the stair,	(count on two fingers)
We worked all night for a scare.	(say "Boo")
When the puppies came by	(creep fingers and knock on door)
Our looks made them shy;	(hide eyes shyly)
Blow out my candle if you dare.	(blow on tip of index finger)
One spooky pumpkin on the stair,	(count on one finger)
I worked all night for a scare.	(say "Boo")
When the princess came by	(creep fingers and knock on door)
My look made her shy;	(hide eyes shyly)
Blow out my candle if you dare.	(blow on tip of finger)

147

Trick-or-Treating

Materials: appliance boxes, bowls of small manipulatives, Halloween costumes, plastic pumpkin pails or candy bags

Create a neighborhood by decorating the appliance boxes to represent houses. If desired, let students help. Place small manipulatives in a bowl inside each "house." Let some students pretend to be homeowners and some pretend to be trick-or-treaters. Have the trick-or-treaters dress in Halloween costumes while the homeowners crawl into the houses to distribute treats. As trick-or-treaters approach each house, they should knock and say, "Trick or treat." Remind students to thank the homeowners after they are given treats. Have students trade places so that everyone gets a chance to trick-or-treat.

Pumpkin Seed Math

Materials: orange paper, scissors, dried or roasted pumpkin seeds, cups

Copy and cut out a pumpkin shape on orange paper for each student. Put small handfuls of dried or roasted pumpkin seeds in cups. Give a cup to each student along with a paper pumpkin. Ask students to count their seeds. Tell them how many seeds to place on the pumpkin shape. Practice simple addition and subtraction as you tell them to add or take away seeds and count their totals each time.

Mayflower Soap Boats

Materials: construction paper or card stock, scissors, toothpicks, tape, floating bath soaps, sensory table, water

Cut several rectangle sails from construction paper or card stock. They should be about the same size as a bar of soap. Laminate each sail for durability. Tape a toothpick to each rectangle. Press each toothpick into a bar of soap to make a boat. Fill the sensory table with water. Let students carefully float the soap boats in the water. Encourage students to blow gently on the sails to push the boats across the water. Have them count how many times they have to blow to move a boat from one side of the table to the other.

Hand-Painted Turkeys

Materials: Turkey Pattern (page 155), scissors, brown construction paper or card stock, several colors of tempera paint, aluminum pie pans, glue, white paper

Make a copy of the Turkey Pattern. Cut it out without the feet. Trace the pattern onto brown construction paper for each student. Or, copy the pattern onto brown card stock. Cut out the turkeys. Pour a thin layer of each paint color into a different aluminum pie pan. Place the supplies on a table. Help students glue the Turkey Patterns onto white paper. Then, let each student press one palm into an aluminum pan of paint. Instruct her to press her two palms together to spread the paint to the tips of her fingers and then make handprints on her paper to create turkey feathers. After she washes her hands, let her choose another color and continue creating feathers. To make feet for the turkey, have her dip her palms into orange paint and spread the paint to the tips of her fingers. Then, she should hold her fingers close together with the thumbs extended to make prints on her paper. Finally, she should add eyes by making two fingerprints with dark paint.

Turkey Feather Count

Materials: Turkey Pattern (page 155), crayons and markers, scissors, 5 plastic foam balls (each 6" [15 cm] in diameter), glue, stiff feathers (available at craft stores)

Make 10 copies of the Turkey Pattern. Write numbers from 1 to 10 on the Turkey Patterns. Color as desired and cut out the turkeys. Fold each turkey so that its feet and the bottom fourth of its body are resting on the table. (See illustration.) Cut the 5 balls in half. Remove a slice at the bottom of each half to create a flat base. Glue each turkey to a plastic foam piece. Each turkey will now sit upright. Arrange the 10 turkeys in random order on a table. Place the feathers on the table as well. Have each student read the number on a turkey and insert that number of "tail feathers" into the plastic foam ball. When he has added the correct number of tail feathers for all of the turkeys, have him remove them so that the next player can take a turn.

Variation: Instead of writing numbers on the turkeys, write simple math sentences for students to solve. Have them insert the number of feathers that corresponds to each answer. Or, draw color patterns for students to match and repeat with colorful feathers.

 (See page 2.)

Ten Turkeys

Have students perform this rhyme as they chant it with you.

Ten Turkeys

Ten turkeys strutted across the road.
One turkey lifted its head and crowed,
Gobble, gobble, gobble, gobble.
The turkeys kept up their wobble.
As I watched them walk back to the wood,
I knew that those turkeys were feeling good.
Another Thanksgiving had passed them by,
For another year, they needn't be shy.

Native American Drums

Materials: I undecorated coffee can per student, brown construction paper or paper grocery bags, scissors, glue, crayons or markers, feathers (available at craft stores), sequins

Provide each student with a lidded coffee can. Cut brown construction paper or paper grocery bags into rectangles to wrap around the empty coffee cans. Glue the paper around the drum. Place the drums and other supplies on a table. Have each student decorate a drum using crayons, markers, feathers, and sequins. Encourage students to use repeating patterns and geometric shapes in their decorations. Let the glue dry. When the drums are dry, tell students to play rhythms by tapping the drums with their hands. Suggest experimenting with how to make different sounds by tapping on the sides of the drums, and using their fingers or palms.

 **(See page 2.)**

Hanukkah Greeting Cards

Materials: construction paper; tissue paper; scissors; glue; crayons and markers; card decorating supplies, such as glitter, stickers, and decorative hole punches

Cut eight strips of colorful construction paper, each approximately 1/2" x 3" (1.25 cm x 7.5 cm), for each student. Cut yellow, red, and orange tissue paper into small squares, approximately 3" x 3" (7.5 cm x 7.5 cm). Fold sheets of construction paper in half to prepare a card for each student. Place the supplies on a table. Have each student glue eight "candles" in a row on the front of her card. Let students use tissue paper squares to make a "flame" for each candle by wrinkling a few squares into a ball and gluing the ball to the top of a candle. Let students decorate their cards as they wish. When the glue is dry, help them write messages on their cards. On the fronts of the cards, students may wish to write words such as *Hanukkah, Love, Lights,* or their names, by placing one letter on each candle. Let students dictate messages to write inside the cards and then present them to family or friends.

Hanukkah Dreidel

Materials: square box, paper, tape, marker

Explain that children play with the dreidel, a top-like toy, when celebrating the Jewish holiday of Hanukkah. The dreidel has four sides. Each side has a Hebrew character printed on it. Depending on which side is showing when the dreidel stops spinning, the person spinning is supposed to perform certain activities. Make a dreidel by covering a square box with paper. Print the four Hebrew characters Nun, Gimmel, Hey, and Shin, one on each side of the box. Print *roll again* on the top and bottom of the box. Have students sit in a large circle. Begin by having one student roll the "dreidel die." In the traditional dreidel game, a certain number of tokens are traded for each Hebrew character. For the purpose of this game, use these actions for the four Hebrew characters:

Nun: The girls walk the circle.

Gimmel: The boys walk the circle.

Hey: The girls walk the circle backward.

Nun   **Gimmel**   **Hey**   **Shin**

Shin: The boys walk the circle backward.

For instance, assume that a *Nun* is rolled. All of the girls should walk around the outside of the circle and return to where they started while the class sings the dreidel song. Try creating different actions for each Hebrew character.

Santa's Sleigh

Materials: large box, masking tape, assortment of toys from the room, large garbage bags

Divide the class into small teams. Place a large box at one end of the room to represent Santa's sleigh and mark a starting line with masking tape on the opposite side of the room. Load an assortment of toys from the room into two large garbage bags. Give a bag to each team, making sure that there is an equal number of toys in each bag. Set these bags on the starting line across from the large box. At your signal, the first player on each team should grab one toy from his team's bag and race to place it in the "sleigh" on the opposite side of the room. The player should then race to the starting line and tag the next student in line. Continue the relay until the sleigh is full and the toy bags are empty.

Hook Horns

Materials: small hoops (can be made with newspaper and tape)

Use a small plastic hoop or create one by rolling a sheet of newspaper on the diagonal and taping the ends together in a loop. Divide the class into pairs. Give each team of "reindeer" their own hoop. Tell them that their arms are their antlers. As one team member tosses the hoop, the other team member should try to catch it on one of her "antlers." Now, have players switch roles.

Leaping Lessons

Materials: masking tape, blocks, small storage boxes

Mark a starting line with a piece of masking tape. Have the little "reindeer" in the class form a line behind the starting line. Have them take turns standing on the line and leaping forward to see who can leap the farthest. Play again and see who can beat his first try. Now, place several obstacles, such as blocks or small storage boxes, around the room and have the reindeer leap through the obstacle course.

Decorating for Christmas

Materials: large box of assorted Christmas decorations, artificial Christmas tree, boxes, wrapping paper, clear tape, bows, gift tags, small toys from the classroom

Place a large box of Christmas decorations in the home living center. Display the Christmas tree. Create a gift-wrapping station on a table. Encourage students to decorate the home center for the holiday. Let them decorate the tree, string tinsel or garland around the center, and wrap "gifts" (small classroom toys) for their classmates and place them under the tree.

Santa's Workshop

Materials: table and chairs, elf hats (purchased or made from construction paper rolled into cones), aprons, toys, paintbrushes, boxes, ribbons, bows, toy tools, wagon, Santa hat and coat, small pillow, reindeer antler headbands (available at discount stores or made from construction paper), large duffel bag, large Christmas stockings

Create Santa's workshop in the dramatic play center. Provide a table and chairs for "elves" to make and paint toys. Provide a second area for putting toys in boxes and tying with bows. Turn a wagon into Santa's sleigh that will be pulled by a "reindeer." Use the small pillow to give Santa a big belly. Help students select the roles that they will play in Santa's workshop. Encourage students to "build" toys, wrap them, load all of the gifts into Santa's duffel bag, put it on the sleigh, and help Santa deliver the gifts by placing them in the stockings.

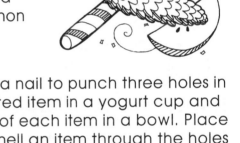

Christmas Smells

Materials: yogurt cups; Christmas stickers; nail; scented items such as fresh pinecones or pine needles, cinnamon sticks, oranges, peppermint, hot chocolate mix, and vanilla spices; tape; bowls

Decorate empty, clean yogurt cups with stickers. Use a nail to punch three holes in the lids of the cups. Put a small amount of each scented item in a yogurt cup and secure the lid in place with tape. Put a small amount of each item in a bowl. Place the cups and bowls on a table. Have each student smell an item through the holes in a yogurt cup and then find the matching scent in one of the bowls. Let students match all of the scents.

 **(See page 2.)**

Ring in a Happy New Year

Materials: small jingle bells, 4 chenille stems per student

Ring in the New Year with a bell-ringing bonanza. String three or four small jingle bells onto a chenille stem. Make four chenille-bell stems for each student. Loosely twist the chenille stems onto each student's ankles and wrists. Have them practice jingling the bells loudly, softly, quickly, and slowly. Let them jingle on their right sides and then on their left sides. Have them jingle with their hands over their heads, straight out to their sides, and behind their backs. Now, let them jingle just their feet, first one and then the other. See if students can move their bodies or walk across the room without making any jingle bell noises.

Valentine Factory

Materials: colorful construction paper; scissors; stapler; hole punch; envelopes; valentine-making supplies, such as crayons, sequins, ribbon, doilies, and glue; ride-on toy car; canvas shoulder bag; 10 storage bins or shoe boxes

Cut out a large supply of hearts from construction paper. Make "cupid hats" for the factory workers by stapling heart cutouts to headbands of construction paper. Establish a "time clock" area where workers will "punch in and out" when entering and leaving the factory. Write each student's name on a paper heart and put it in an envelope at the entrance to the "factory." Place the hole punch near the envelope. Arrange an assembly table in the "factory" with all of the valentine supplies in an assembly line. Create a delivery vehicle by decorating the ride-on toy car with hearts. Number the bins or shoe boxes from 1 to 10 and place them around the perimeter of the "factory" to represent 10 neighborhood mailboxes. When students enter, they should find their hearts and "punch in" with the hole punch. Then, they should put on their cupid hats and begin assembling valentines! Encourage students to put the valentines in envelopes and write a number from 1 to 10 to "address" each envelope. When a batch is complete, a student should act as the delivery person and put the valentines in the canvas bag. She should "drive" from one mailbox to another to deliver the numbered valentines to the corresponding mailboxes. Have students take turns so that everyone gets a chance to be the delivery person.

Saint Patrick's Day Pot-of-Gold Hunt

Materials: gold construction paper, scissors, permanent marker

Make lots of gold coins by drawing 2" (5 cm) circles on the construction paper. Laminate the circles for durability and cut them out. With a permanent marker, write the numbers 1 to 5 on the coins so that each coin has one number written on it. Hide the coins, number side down, around the room. Have students sit close to you. Tell them that you are a lucky leprechaun who has hidden your gold coins for good little boys and girls. Each student should then raise his hand and ask the Lucky Leprechaun for permission to look for a coin by saying, "Lucky Leprechaun, may I hunt for gold?" Respond by acknowledging his wish, but explain that he must follow your directions. For example, you might say, "Yes, but you must take baby steps." The student should then baby step around the room until he finds a coin. Then, he should return to the circle to await his next turn. When all students have taken turns finding gold coins, play again using the numbers on the coins that they found during the first round. This time, when a student is acknowledged, has asked politely, and has been given a movement challenge, she should try to find the number of coins indicated on the first coin she found.

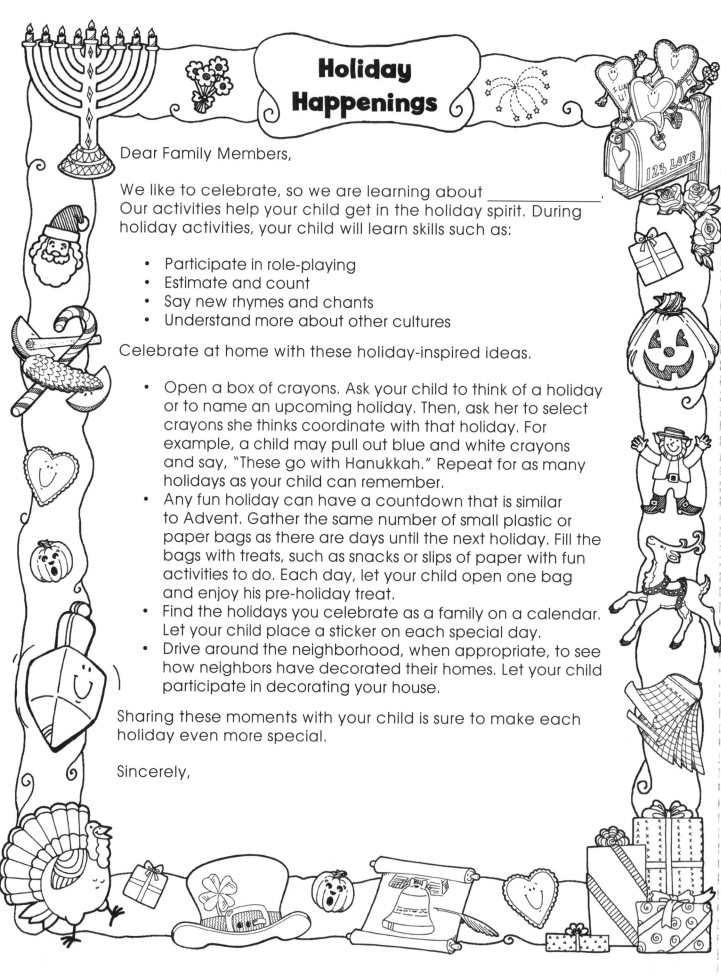

Holiday Happenings

Dear Family Members,

We like to celebrate, so we are learning about _____.
Our activities help your child get in the holiday spirit. During holiday activities, your child will learn skills such as:

- Participate in role-playing
- Estimate and count
- Say new rhymes and chants
- Understand more about other cultures

Celebrate at home with these holiday-inspired ideas.

- Open a box of crayons. Ask your child to think of a holiday or to name an upcoming holiday. Then, ask her to select crayons she thinks coordinate with that holiday. For example, a child may pull out blue and white crayons and say, "These go with Hanukkah." Repeat for as many holidays as your child can remember.
- Any fun holiday can have a countdown that is similar to Advent. Gather the same number of small plastic or paper bags as there are days until the next holiday. Fill the bags with treats, such as snacks or slips of paper with fun activities to do. Each day, let your child open one bag and enjoy his pre-holiday treat.
- Find the holidays you celebrate as a family on a calendar. Let your child place a sticker on each special day.
- Drive around the neighborhood, when appropriate, to see how neighbors have decorated their homes. Let your child participate in decorating your house.

Sharing these moments with your child is sure to make each holiday even more special.

Sincerely,

All the World by Liz Garton Scanlon (Beach Lane Books, 2009)

Amazing Airplanes by Tony Mitton and Ant Parker (Kingfisher, 2005)

Animals in the Fall by Gail Saunders-Smith (Capstone Press, 2000)

Baa Baa Black Sheep by Iza Trapani (Charlesbridge Publishing, 2001)

Bear's New Friend by Karma Wilson (Simon & Schuster, 2006)

The Best Pet of All by David LaRochelle (Dutton Juvenile, 2004)

Birds, Nests and Eggs by Mel Boring (NorthWord Books for Young Readers, 1998)

Birthday Pet by Ellen Javernick (Marshall Cavendish Corporation, 2009)

Boo Hoo Bird by Jeremy Tankard (Scholastic, 2009)

Butternut Hollow Pond by Brian J. Heinz (First Avenue Editions, 2005)

Circus by Lois Ehlert (HarperCollins, 1992)

The Circus Ship by Chris Van Dusen (Candlewick Press, 2009)

Classic Nursery Rhymes by Paige Weber (Gramercy, 2006)

Cleo's Color Book by Stella Blackstone (Barefoot Books, 2010)

Click, Clack, Moo: Cows That Type by Doreen Cronin (Simon & Schuster Children's Publishing, 2000)

The Cloud Book by Tomie de Paola (Holiday House, 1984)

Cloudy With a Chance of Meatballs by Judi Barrett (Aladdin, 1982)

Color Me a Rhyme: Nature Poems for Young People by Jane Yolen (Boyds Mills Press, 2003)

A Color of His Own by Leo Lionni (Knopf Books for Young Readers, 2006)

The Colors of Us by Karen Katz (Henry Holt and Co. BYR Paperbacks, 2007)

Come On, Rain! by Karen Hesse (Scholastic, 1999)

The Completed Hickory Dickory Dock by Jim Aylesworth (Aladdin, 1994)

Crickwing by Janell Cannon (Sandpiper, 2005)

Danny and the Dinosaur by Syd Hoff (HarperCollins, 1958)

The Day Jimmy's Boa Ate the Wash by Trinka Hakes Noble (Puffin, 1992)

Dinosaur Roar! by Paul Stickland and Henrietta Stickland (Puffin, 2002)

Farm Animals by DK Publishing (DK Publishing, 2004)

Feathers for Lunch by Lois Ehlert (Sandpiper, 1996)

Felicity Floo Visits the Zoo by E. S. Redmond (Candlewick Press, 2009)

The First Day of Winter by Denise Fleming (Henry Holt and Co., 2005)

Foo, the Flying Frog of Washtub Pond by Belle Yang (Candlewick Press, 2009)

Franklin Wants a Pet by Paulette Bourgeois (Scholastic Paperbacks, 1995)

From Seed to Plant by Gail Gibbons (Holiday House, 1993)

Good Night, Gorilla by Peggy Rathmann (Putnam Juvenile, 1996)

The Grumpy Dump Truck by Brie Spangler (Knopf Books for Young Readers, 2009)

Higher! Higher! by Leslie Patricelli (Candlewick Press, 2009)

A House for Hermit Crab by Eric Carle (Aladdin, 2005)

How Are You Peeling? by Joost Elffers and Saxton Freymann (Scholastic Paperbacks, 2004)

How Big Were the Dinosaurs? by Bernard Most (Sandpiper, 1995)

How Do Dinosaurs Love Their Cats? by Jane Yolen (The Blue Sky Press, 2010)

How Do Dinosaurs Say Good Night? by Jane Yolen (Blue Sky Press, 2000)

How I Spent My Summer Vacation by Mark Teague (Dragonfly Books, 1997)

Hurray for Today!: All about Holidays by Bonnie Worth (Random House Books for Young Readers, 2004)

I Like Myself! by Karen Beaumont (Harcourt Children's Books, 2004)

I Stink! by Kate McMullan (HarperCollins, 2006)

The Icky Bug Counting Book by Jerry Pallotta (Charlesbridge Publishing, 1992)

If I Ran the Circus by Dr. Seuss (Random House Books for Young Readers, 1956)

I'm Gonna Like Me: Letting Off a Little Self-Esteem by Jamie Lee Curtis (HarperCollins, 2002)

I'm the Biggest Thing in the Ocean by Kevin Sherry (Dial, 2007)

In the Small, Small Pond by Denise Fleming (Henry Holt and Co. BYR Paperbacks, 2007)

Inside a Barn in the Country by Alyssa Satin Capucilli (Scholastic, 1995)

Into the A, B, Sea: An Ocean Alphabet Book by Deborah Lee Rose (Scholastic, 2000)

It Looked Like Spilt Milk by Charles G. Shaw (HarperFestival, 1992)

It's Fall by Linda Glaser (Millbrook Press, 2001)

It's Pumpkin Time! by Zoe Hall (Scholastic Paperbacks, 1999)

It's Spring! by Linda Glaser (Millbrook Press, 2002)

Jack and Jill by Salley Mavor (Houghton Mifflin, 2006)

Jack's Garden by Henry Cole (Greenwillow Books, 1997)

Just a Day at the Pond by Mercer Mayer (HarperFestival, 2008)

Last Night I Dreamed a Circus by Maya Gottfried (Knopf Books for Young Readers, 2003)

Leaf Man by Lois Ehlert (Harcourt Children's Books, 2005)

Little Bear's Little Boat by Eve Bunting (Clarion Books, 2003)

Little Bird, Biddle Bird by David Kirk (Scholastic Press, 2001)

The Little Engine That Could by Watty Piper (Grosset & Dunlap, 1990)

Little Red's Autumn Adventure by Sarah The Duchess of York Ferguson (Simon & Schuster Children's Publishing, 2009)

Miss Spider's Tea Party by David Kirk (Scholastic, 2007)

The Mitten by Jan Brett (Scholastic, 1990)

Moishe's Miracle: A Hanukkah Story by Laura Krauss Melmed (HarperCollins, 2000)

Mrs. Wishy-Washy's Farm by Joy Cowley (Puffin, 2006)

My Big Dinosaur Book by Roger Priddy (St. Martin's Press, 2004)

My Spring Robin by Anne Rockwell (Aladdin, 1996)

My Visit to the Zoo by Aliki (HarperCollins, 1999)

The Night Before Christmas by Clement C. Moore (HarperCollins, 2004)

One Hot Summer Day by Nina Crews (Greenwillow, 1995)

A Penguin Story by Antoinette Portis (HarperCollins, 2008)

The Perfect Pet by Margie Palatini (Katherine Tegen Books, 2003)

Pet Show! by Ezra Jack Keats (Puffin, 2001)

Planting a Rainbow by Lois Ehlert (Sandpiper, 1992)

Red Sings from Treetops: A Year in Colors by Joyce Sidman (Houghton Mifflin Books for Children, 2009)

Room for a Little One: A Christmas Tale by Martin Waddell (Margaret K. McElderry, 2006)

See the Circus by H. A. Rey (Houghton Mifflin, 1998)

A Seed Grows: My First Look at a Plant's Life Cycle by Pamela Hickman (Kids Can Press, 1997)

Seven Spools of Thread: A Kwanzaa Story by Angela Shelf Medearis (Albert Whitman & Company, 2000)

Snow by Uri Shulevitz (Farrar, Straus and Giroux, 2004)

The Snowflake: A Water Cycle Story by Neil Waldman (Millbrook Press, 2003)

The Snowy Day by Ezra Jack Keats (Puffin, 1976)

Spring Is Here by Taro Gomi (Chronicle Books, 2006)

Summer by Alice Low (Random House Books for Young Readers, 2001)

Summer Stinks by Marty Kelley (Zino Press Children's Books, 2001)

Swimmy by Leo Lionni (Dragonfly Books, 1973)

Tacky the Penguin by Helen Lester (Houghton Mifflin, 1990)

Thanksgiving Is for Giving Thanks by Margaret Sutherland (Grosset & Dunlap, 2000)

This Is My Body by Gina and Mercer Mayer (Golden Books, 2000)

To Be Like the Sun by Susan Marie Swanson (Harcourt Children's Books, 2008)

Tracks in the Snow by Wong Herbert Yee (Square Fish, 2007)

Trick or Treat? by John Bianchi (Grosset & Dunlap, 2002)

The Very Hungry Caterpillar by Eric Carle (Philomel, 1981)

The Very Ugly Bug by Liz Pichon (Tiger Tales, 2007)

We Are All Alike . . . We Are All Different by The Cheltenham Elementary School Kindergartners (Scholastic Paperbacks, 2002)

Weather Words and What They Mean by Gail Gibbons (Holiday House, 1992)

Wee Willie Winkie by Salley Mavor (Houghton Mifflin, 2006)

What's in the Pond? (Hidden Life) by Anne Hunter (Sandpiper, 1999)

The Wheels on the Bus by Paul O. Zelinsky (Dutton Juvenile, 1990)

When will it be spring? by Catherine Walters (Little Tiger Press, 1998)

White Rabbit's Color Book by Alan Baker (Kingfisher, 1999)

Who Sank the Boat? by Pamela Allen (Putnam Juvenile, 1996)

You See a Circus. I See... by Mike Downs (Charlesbridge Publishing, 2006)

Zoo-Looking by Mem Fox (Mondo Publishing, 1996)

Zoo-ology by Joëlle Jolivet (Roaring Brook Press, 2003)